QUESTIONS FOR GCSE PHYSICS

Nick England
David Harrison

THE KING'S SCHOOL, CANTERBURY
PHYSICS DEPARTMENT

D1147830

Hodder & Stoughton

A MEMBER OF THE HODDER HEADLINE GROUP

Preface

All subjects taken at GCSE level require you to master a broad framework of knowledge, to have understanding of principles and to develop the skills to solve problems or to deal with unfamiliar situations. This is certainly the case with Physics, where a good student must have the confidence in his or her understanding of quite complex principles to be able to tackle unusual problems.

Questions for GCSE Physics has been written as a companion to Physics Matters (ISBN 0 340 639350), though the book could easily be used on its own or as a supplement to any standard textbook. Each chapter of problems corresponds to a chapter in Physics Matters. While Physics Matters concentrates on providing knowledge and understanding, Questions for GCSE Physics provides you with a full range of practice questions, which set out to test recall of knowledge and improve problem-solving skills so that you can tackle your exams with confidence. To help jog memories, brief summaries of essential information are provided in each section and selected answers to the questions are available separately (ISBN 0 340 712104).

Nick England
David Harrison
1997

Acknowledgements

The publishers would like to thank the following artists who drew the illustrations: Jeff Edwards, Mike Feeney of Red Herring Design and Illustration, Phil Ford and Peters & Zabransky.

We are grateful to the following companies and institutions who have given permission to reproduce photographs in this book: NASA/Science Photo Library (21 top); US Geological Survey/Science Photo Library (21 bottom).

A catalogue record for this title is available from the British Library

ISBN 0 340 688289

First published 1997
Impression number   10   9   8   7   6   5   4
Year   2004   2003

Typeset by Wearset, Boldon, Tyne and Wear
Printed in Great Britain for Hodder & Stoughton Educational, a division of Hodder Headline Ltd., 338 Euston Road, London NW1 3BH by J. W. Arrowsmith Ltd., Bristol.

Contents

1 Forces

Density and pressure

$$\text{Density} = \frac{\text{mass}}{\text{volume}}$$

Density is usually measured in units of kg/m³.

$$\text{Pressure} = \frac{\text{force}}{\text{area}} \qquad P = \frac{F}{A}$$

Pressure is measured in N/m² or Pascal (Pa).

Questions

1 A student wrote the following sentence in an exam paper; read it and correct any mistakes.

'A cork floats in a pond because it is lighter than water; a stone sinks because it is too heavy to float in any liquid.'

2 Copy and complete Table 1.

Metal	Volume (m³)	Mass (kg)	Density (kg/m³)
gold		386	19 300
lead	0.4	4560	
steel	2	16 000	
titanium	0.5		4500
aluminium	3		2700
mercury		68	13 600

Table 1

3 Gold can be hammered out into a very thin foil. Calculate the mass of gold required to make a foil 0.001 mm thick, 10 cm long and 10 cm wide. The density of gold is 19.3 g/cm³.

4 A gas cylinder is described as 'empty' when the pressure in it is 1 atmosphere. A full cylinder has gas in it at a pressure of 10 atmospheres.

A cylinder used for storing carbon dioxide has a mass of 9.5 kg when 'empty'. The volume of carbon dioxide is 0.1 m³. Calculate the mass of the cylinder when full. You need to know that the density of carbon dioxide is 2.0 kg/m³ at a pressure of 1 atmosphere (at room temperature).

5 Use the idea of pressure to explain the following.

a) A saw has a jagged edge.

b) A knife cuts better when sharpened.

c) You should not walk over a wooden floor in stiletto heels.

d) Canadians wear snow shoes to get about in winter.

e) A tank has caterpillar tracks on it.

6 Figure 1 parts A, B and C shows three boxes. Which box would you use, and how would you position it, to exert (i) the smallest pressure on the ground and (ii) the largest pressure on the ground?

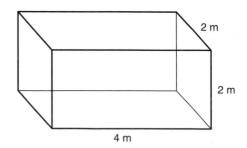

A   Weight = 18 000 N

2 m

2 m

4 m

Figure 1A

2

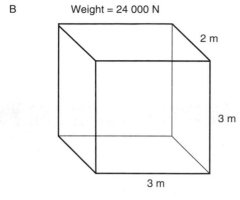

B Weight = 24 000 N

2 m

3 m

3 m

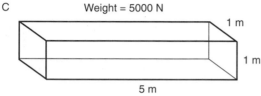

C Weight = 5000 N

1 m

1 m

5 m

Figure 1B and C

	Weight of girl (N)	Area of heel of shoe (cm²)
Amanda	800	4
Brenda	600	1
Chloe	600	2
Denise	400	4
Elinor	400	1

Table 2

9 a) Table 3 below shows the pressure underneath the sea's surface. Plot a graph of pressure (y-axis) against depth (x-axis).

Pressure (kPa)	120	140	160	180	200
Depth (m)	2	4	6	8	10

Table 3

7 a) Figure 2 shows a piece of glass being lifted by a suction cup. The area of the cup is 0.005 m² and the pressure in the cup has been reduced to 0.7 atmospheres. (1 atmosphere pressure = 100 000 Pa.) What is the greatest weight you could lift safely with this cup?

   b) What possible changes could you make to lift a larger piece of glass safely?

   b) Use your graph to predict the pressure at (i) 5 m depth (ii) 20 m depth (iii) at the sea's surface.

   c) The box in Figure 3 is held so that its top is 2 m below the surface.
   i) Calculate the force exerted on the top of the box by the water.
   ii) Calculate the force exerted on the bottom of the box by the water.

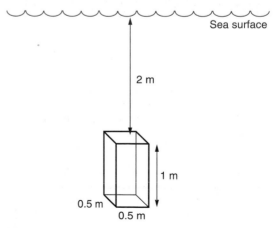

Sea surface

2 m

1 m

0.5 m

0.5 m

Figure 3

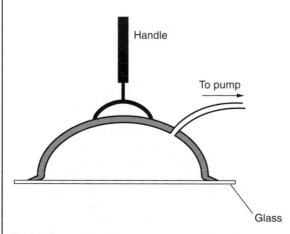

Handle

To pump

Glass

Figure 2

8 Five girls stand on one heel of their shoes (Table 2). Which girl puts the greatest pressure on the floor?

   iii) The box has a weight of 2000 N. Will it float?
   iv) Explain whether a box of weight 3000 N, of the same volume, would float.

3

10 Figure 4 shows a mercury barometer.

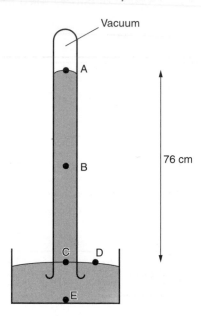

Figure 4

a) What can you say about the pressure at A?

b) The pressure at D is 100 kPa. What is the pressure at C?

c) Which point is under the greatest pressure?

11 Figure 5 shows the principle of a hydraulic jack.

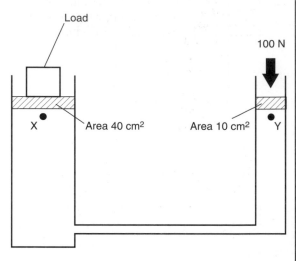

Figure 5

a) What pressure is exerted by the 100 N force at Y?

b) How big is the pressure at X?

c) Calculate the maximum load which can be lifted by the 100 N force.

d) To lift the load by 10 cm how far do you have to move with the applied 100 N force?

Forces

- ▶ A force is a push or a pull.
- ▶ A force can stretch or squash something.
- ▶ A force can turn something.
- ▶ A force can start or stop something moving.
- ▶ The turning moment of a force is defined by: moment = force × perpendicular distance.

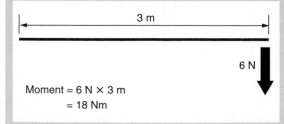

Moment = 6 N × 3 m
 = 18 Nm

- ▶ When a body remains still all the forces on it and turning moment balance. We say the body is in **equilibrium**.

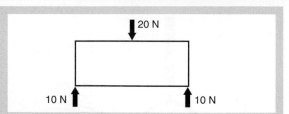

This body is in equilibrium.

- ▶ Some springs obey **Hooke's law** for which the extension of the spring is proportional to the force causing the stretching.
- ▶ Stiff, strong materials, such as steel, are good for building. Concrete is strong when squashed (compressed) but it is weak when stretched.
- ▶ **Forces occur in pairs.** If I push you with a force; you push me back with an equal force in the opposite direction.

Questions

12 Frank's weight is 800 N, and his bike's weight is 2500 N (Figure 6). What upwards force is exerted by the road on the rear wheel?

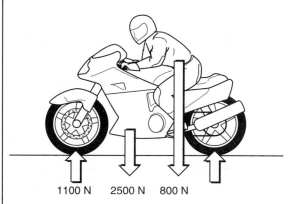

1100 N 2500 N 800 N

Figure 6

13 A man is walking; Figure 7 shows the direction of the force his foot puts on the ground. Copy the diagram, and show the direction of the push on his shoe from the ground.

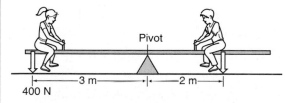

Figure 7

14 a) A boy and a girl sit on a seesaw (Figure 8). It is balanced. What is the boy's weight?

Pivot

3 m ── 2 m

400 N

Figure 8

    b) The seesaw itself has a weight of 300 N. How big is the force which the pivot exerts on the seesaw?

15 Calculate the pull of the spring on the beam shown in Figure 9.

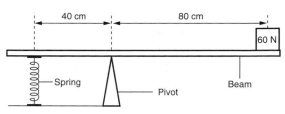

40 cm   80 cm   60 N

Spring   Pivot   Beam

Figure 9

16 a) A fisherman has caught a large fish, and weighs it using two balances (Figure 10). What is the fish's weight?

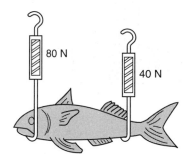

80 N   40 N

Figure 10

    b) A weighbridge is to be used to measure the weight of a large lorry with four axles, weight 90 000 N. The weighbridge is small and can only measure up to 30 000 N. Describe how you would measure the weight of this lorry.

17 In Figure 11, an 8 N weight is supported by a beam, which is itself supported by two spring balances (A and B). What does each spring balance read?

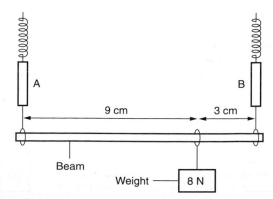

A   9 cm   3 cm   B

Beam   Weight ── 8 N

Figure 11

18 A box labelled X, with mass 0.1 kg, is hung from a spring; the extension is 3 cm. In Figure 12, other boxes are hanging from arrangements of similar springs. Calculate the mass of boxes A–D.

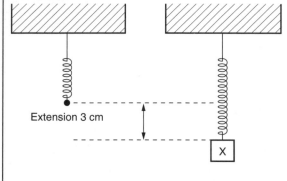

Extension 3 cm

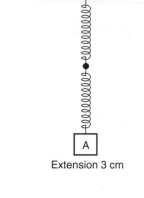

A — Extension 3 cm

B — Extension 6 cm

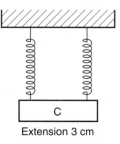

C — Extension 3 cm

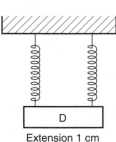

D — Extension 1 cm

Figure 12

19 Table 4 shows how a steel spring extends when increasing loads are hung on it.

Load (N)	1.0	2.0	3.0	4.0	4.5	5.0
Extension (cm)	2.0	4.0	6.0	8.0	10.0	12.0

Table 4

 a) Plot a graph of extension (y-axis) against load (x-axis).

 b) Up to what load does the spring obey Hooke's law?

 c) What happens to the spring when a load of 5 N has been put on it?

20 What is the reading on the spring balance in Figure 13?

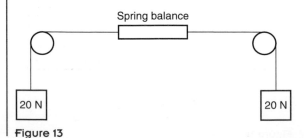

Spring balance

20 N   20 N

Figure 13

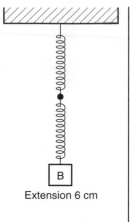

Concrete roadway

Concrete pillar

Figure 14

21 a) Figure 14 shows a concrete bridge. Make a sketch of the concrete roadway, and mark which parts are under compression (C) and which parts are under tension (T).

 b) Concrete bridges need to be reinforced. Why is ordinary concrete not used? Explain how the concrete is reinforced.

22 a) What is meant by the centre of gravity of a body?

b) In Figure 15 which wooden block is
i) most likely to topple
ii) least likely to topple?

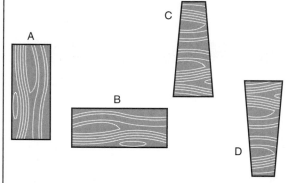

Figure 15

23 Where is the centre of gravity of the block in Figure 16? The block has a weight of 15 N.

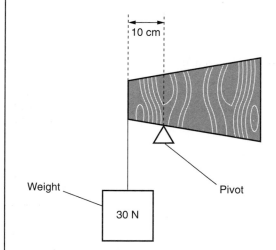

Figure 16

24 Figure 17 shows how the lengths of a steel spring and a rubber band vary when forces are applied to them.

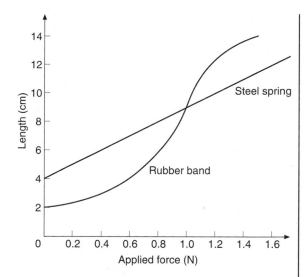

Figure 17

a) Which one obeys Hooke's law over the region investigated?

b) The spring and band are now placed in series as in Figure 18A. What is the total length of this arrangement when a force of 0.8 N is applied?

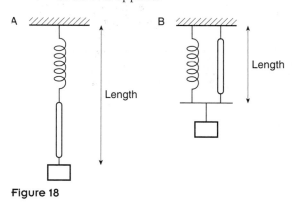

Figure 18

c) The springs are now arranged in parallel as in Figure 18B. What force must be applied to produce a length of (i) 9 cm, (ii) 4 cm?

d) What length does arrangement B have when the force applied is 1.3 N?

7

2 Motion and its Measurement

Distance, velocity and acceleration

▶ Average speed = $\dfrac{\text{distance}}{\text{time}}$

▶ We often use the term 'speed' instead of 'velocity'. However, when used correctly velocity must also include a direction. For example: a car has a velocity of 20 m/s due west; its speed is 20 m/s.

▶ Acceleration = $\dfrac{\text{change of velocity}}{\text{time}}$

▶ The units of acceleration are usually written as m/s². It is easier to understand if you write 'm/s per second': this reminds you that an acceleration of 2 m/s per second means that something is increasing its speed by 2 m/s every second.

▶ Deceleration is a *negative* acceleration.

▶ When something accelerates at a constant rate from a speed u to a speed v, its average speed is:

Average speed = $\dfrac{u + v}{2}$

▶ Distance–time graphs
  a) constant speed

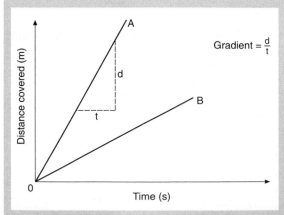

The gradient = speed. A is travelling faster than B.

  b) changing speed

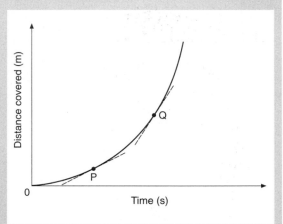

Now something is accelerating. It is travelling faster at Q than at P; the gradient is steeper at Q.

▶ Velocity–time graphs

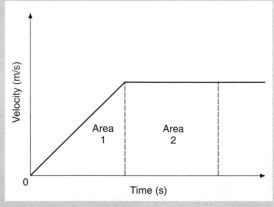

The gradient of a velocity–time graph = acceleration. The area under the graph = distance covered.

Questions

1 Table 1 shows average speeds and times recorded by top athletes in several track events. Copy and complete the table.

Event	Average speed (m/s)	Time
100 m		10.0 s
200 m	10.3	
400 m	8.9	
	7.1	3 m 30 s
10 000 m		29 m 10 s
	5.7	2 h 8 m 2 s

Table 1

2 Sam, a sculler, goes on a training session on the river. First she rows 4 km upstream, which takes 1 hour; and then she returns back downstream, which takes her 30 minutes.

a) Calculate her average speed for (i) the upstream trip (ii) the downstream trip.

b) Calculate her average speed for the whole trip. (*Hint*: the answer is *not* 6 km/h.)

c) Calculate the speed of the river current, assuming that Sam rowed at the same rate in both directions.

3 A Saturn V rocket accelerates at an average rate of 3 m/s^2 for 2 minutes after take off. Work out its speed after 2 minutes flying time.

4 A car is travelling at 30 m/s. The driver takes his foot off the accelerator and slows down. His deceleration is 2 m/s^2. How long does it take him to slow to 15 m/s?

5 A fly can take off and reach a speed of 2 m/s in 50 milliseconds: what is its acceleration?

6 Eddie goes for a cycle ride. There are four stages to his journey.
i) Cycling away from home for 1 hour at a speed of 10 km/h.
ii) Cycling away from home for $\frac{1}{2}$ hour at a speed of 20 km/h.
iii) A rest for lunch taking $\frac{1}{2}$ hour.
iv) Cycling home at a constant speed of 15 km/h.

a) Draw a distance–time graph to show how his distance away from home changes during the journey.

b) Show on your graph where he was travelling the fastest, and the time taken for each part of the journey.

7 Figure 1 shows a distance–time graph of how Jane moved over 6 seconds. Draw a velocity–time graph for her movement.

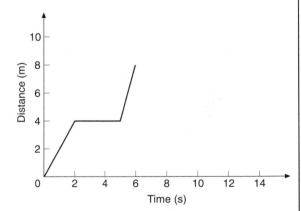

Figure 1

8 Figure 2 shows a velocity–time graph for a short cycle ride.

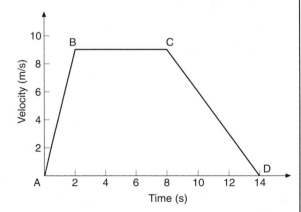

Figure 2

a) Calculate:
i) the acceleration over the region AB
ii) the deceleration over the region CD.

b) Calculate the distance travelled by the cyclist over the 14 seconds.

c) Calculate the average speed.

9

9 Describe how the *velocity* changes in each of the graphs A–F in Figure 3.

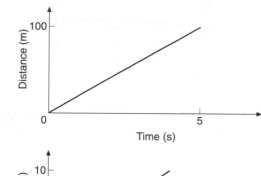

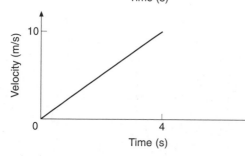

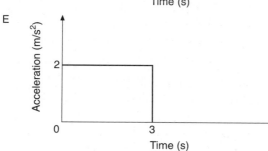

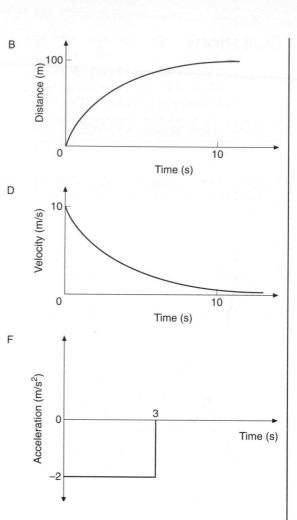

Figure 3

10 Hank is an astronaut who has been given the job of calculating the gravitational acceleration on the asteroid Ceres, our Moon and Mars. He drops a ball-bearing through two pairs of light gates (Figure 4), and measures the time for it to fall using a data logger (Table 2). As the ball passes gate 1A the data logger's clock starts, and as the ball passes each other gate the time taken to reach that point is recorded.

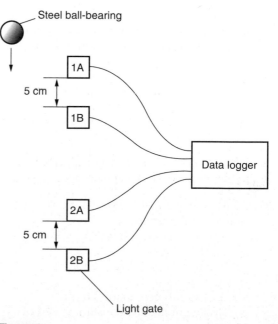

Light gate	Time (ms) (Ceres)	Time (ms) (Moon)	Time (ms) (Mars)
1A	0	0	0
1B	100	50	100
2A	1208	678	657
2B	1253	702	675

Table 2

Note: 1 millisecond (ms) = 0.001 seconds.

Figure 4

a) For Ceres:
i) Work out the average speed of the ball between gates 1A and 1B.
ii) Work out the average speed of the ball between gates 2A and 2B.
iii) Now work out the gravitational acceleration on Ceres.

b) Repeat this process to calculate the gravitational acceleration on our Moon and Mars.

c) Hank does not always drop the ball from the same height above gate 1A. Explain why this does *not* affect his results.

Newton's laws of motion

Forces

▶ Forces can change the motion of a body. For example: Fred is sitting still in his cart. Mandy pushes Fred and he starts to move; we say he increases his speed or accelerates.

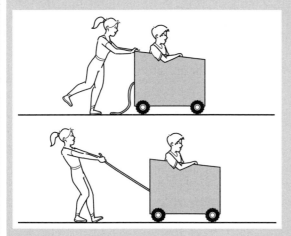

When Fred is moving, Mandy pulls on the rope to slow him down; we say his speed decreases or he decelerates.

▶ A force can also be applied to change the *direction* of motion. For example, a football rolls past you at 3 m/s and you kick it so it still runs at 3 m/s, but in a different direction.

Newton's first law of motion

▶ If no force or two balanced forces act on a body, there is no change in its motion. Examples include:
i) You are sitting in a chair. You stay still because your weight (pull of gravity) is balanced by a push upwards from the chair.
ii) You are freewheeling on your bicycle down a hill. You move at a constant speed when wind resistance balances the pull of gravity down the hill.

Newton's second law of motion

▶ When an unbalanced force acts on you, you accelerate. The size of this acceleration is given by the formula:

force = mass × acceleration

Weight and mass

▶ Your **weight** depends on the strength of the gravitational field. On Earth the gravitational field strength, g, is about 10 N/kg.

Your weight: $W = mg$ m is your mass in kg.

▶ **Mass** is quite hard to define. It is a measure of how hard it is to accelerate a body. A massive object is harder to accelerate than a light object.
For example: you are in outerspace where there is no gravitational pull, so everything is **weightless**. You give a friend two footballs, one of which is filled with concrete. Your friend kicks the hollow one without a problem. He breaks his toe on the one filled with concrete. You explain that he has learned something about mass! The massive (concrete) ball needed a very big force for it to accelerate.

$$mass = \frac{force}{acceleration}$$

Newton's third law of motion

▶ This law states that for every force there is an equal and opposite force.
For example: when you walk, you push the Earth backwards; it pushes you forwards. If the Earth did not push, you would stay where you are. The same idea applies to all motion: when a plane flies, the jet engines push air backwards; the air pushes the plane forwards.

11

Questions

11 In Figure 5 each box is stationary. In each case, describe what will happen when the forces act on the box.

A
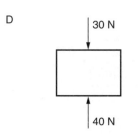

B
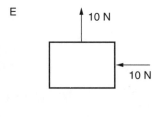

C
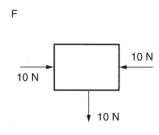

D
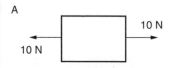

E
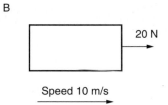

F
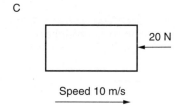

Figure 5

12 In Figure 6 the box is moving to the right at a speed of 10 m/s. Some forces are applied to it again. Describe how these forces affect its motion in A–F. Your answers might include words like 'accelerate', 'decelerate' or phrases like 'changes direction'.

A
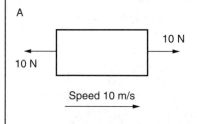

B

C

D
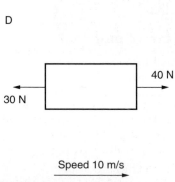

E
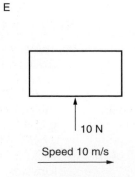

F
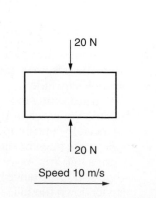

13 a) Angela is a skydiver. In Figure 7A she is falling at a constant speed. How big is the drag force, X, acting on her parachute?

b) In Figure 7B, Angela has just opened her parachute after diving at high speed. Describe how her motion is changing.

A

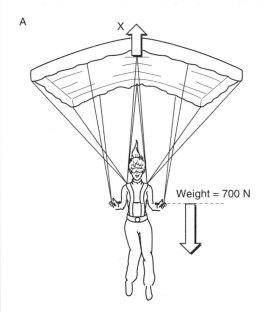

Weight = 700 N

B

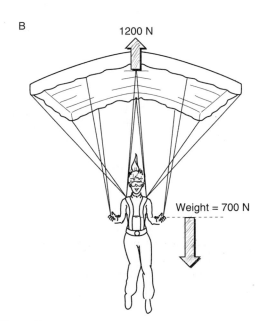

1200 N

Weight = 700 N

Figure 7

14 Work out the accelerations of the three boxes A–C in Figure 8.

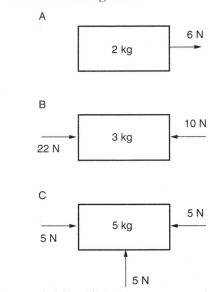

A

2 kg — 6 N

B

22 N → 3 kg ← 10 N

C

5 N → 5 kg ← 5 N

↑ 5 N

Figure 8

15 Andrew is cycling at 5 m/s, and in 5 seconds increases his speed to 7 m/s.

a) Calculate his acceleration.

b) The mass of Andrew and his bicycle is 50 kg. The push forwards from the road on the bicycle is 30 N. Calculate the size of wind resistance, R, acting on him (Figure 9). Assume he has the acceleration calculated in part (a).

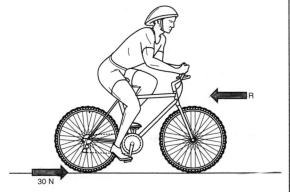

R

30 N

Figure 9

16 You are in outer space, and you are worried that your crew is looking thin. How are you going to work out their mass in a weightless environment? Describe an experiment to calculate an astronaut's mass, using a chair, a large spring balance, a stop clock and a tape measure.

17 Greg test drives his new car. He accelerates rapidly until he reaches a speed of 20 m/s. The mass of the car (with him in it) is 750 kg. Figure 10 shows how his speed changes.

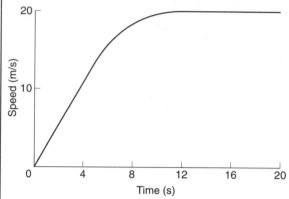

Figure 10

a) Calculate his acceleration over the first 4 seconds.

b) Work out the force acting on the car to accelerate it.

c) Greg invites three friends (total mass 250 kg) into his car to demonstrate its rapid acceleration. Copy Figure 10, and show how the car accelerates over the first 4 seconds. (Label the graph clearly.)

18 This question is about the take off of a lunar landing craft. Use the data provided: mass of craft 20 000 kg; thrust from engines on craft 52 000 N; Moon's gravitational field strength 1.6 N/kg.

a) What is the craft's weight?

b) At take off, calculate the net force on the craft.

c) Calculate the acceleration of the craft at take off.

d) How fast will the craft be travelling after 30 seconds?

e) How far above the Moon's surface will the spacecraft be after 30 seconds?

f) Give two reasons why the craft will actually have travelled slightly further than you estimate.

g) Why could this spacecraft not take off from the surface of the Earth?

19 Jodi and Erica are having a tug of war. Erica is stronger than Jodi and wins. However, Rodney observes that 'since Newton's third law says that Jodi and Erica exert equal but opposite forces on each other, Newton's laws must be wrong sometimes'. Draw diagrams to show the forces acting on the girls, and to explain why Rodney is wrong.

20 The driver of a car leaves a bag of shopping on the passenger seat next to him. During his journey he brakes suddenly. The shopping flies forward off the seat. Explain why.

21 This question is about a mountain bike. You will need to use the information in Figures 11–13.

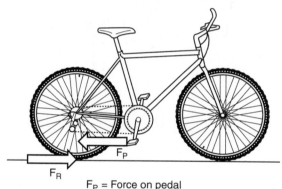

F_P = Force on pedal
F_R = Force from the road on the bike

Figure 11

a) The graph in Figure 12B shows how the resistive forces change with speed for two cyclists.
i) Why is the wind resistance more on the upright cyclist than it is for the crouched cyclist travelling at the same speed?
ii) Why does the wind resistance on a cyclist increase at higher speed?
iii) Figure 12B also shows that the cyclists experience some rolling resistance, due to friction in bearings. How big is that resistive force?

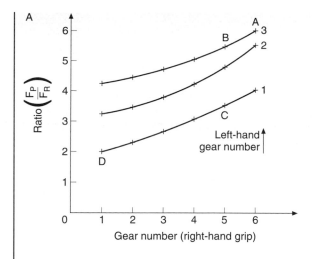

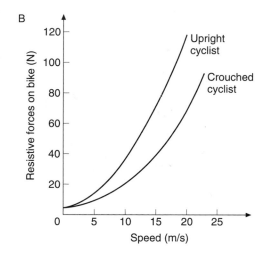

Figure 12

iii) Explain why the cyclist could maintain these speeds in gear A but not gear D.

c) When a cyclist approaches a gradual slope he changes from gear A to gear B. Explain why a cyclist might jump suddenly from gear B to gear C when approaching a steep hill. Now comment on the gearing in the left hand and right hand grips.

d) When you cycle uphill you are working against gravity. When the hill is graded 1 in 5 you have to work against 1/5 of your weight (Figure 13). What extra force do you work against on a hill of gradient 1 in 10?

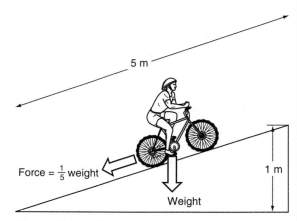

Figure 13 Here the cyclist goes up a 1 in 5 slope – every 5 m along the road you climb 1 m.

A mountain bike has lots of gears, so that you can go along a level road fast, or climb uphill. On a level road, you move quickly against quite a small resistive force; when you go uphill, you have to work hard against gravity. In any case, you are limited by how much power you can produce. A fit cyclist can pedal for half an hour or so, developing a useful power of about 400 W. Your power is related to your speed by the formula:

power = resistive forces × speed

b) i) Show that a cyclist with a power of about 400 W, can cycle in an upright position at a speed of about 10 m/s, along a level road.
ii) What speed can he maintain in the crouched position?

e) Our cyclist approaches an uphill gradient of 1 in 10. His weight (including the bicycle) is 800 N. Show that he can cycle up this hill at a speed of just less than 5 m/s, when in the upright position. (Assume his power is 400 W.)

f) Having got to the top of the hill the cyclist free wheels down the other side, which has a gradient of 1 in 8.
i) What is the maximum speed he can reach in the upright position?
ii) What speed will he reach if he crouches?
iii) Explain why a cyclist would be very foolish to cycle down a 1 in 4 gradient.

15

Momentum

- Momentum = mass × velocity
- Momentum is a **vector quantity**; this means it has a **direction** as well as a **size**. For example you might describe momentum to the right as positive, and momentum to the left as negative.
- $F \times t = m(v - u)$

  Impulse (force × time) = change of momentum

- You can write the units of momentum as either Ns or kg m/s.
- Momentum is a very important quantity because in all collisions or explosions **momentum is conserved**. This means that when two bodies collide the sum of their momentum is the same before the collision as it is afterwards. This allows us to predict what will happen after a collision (or an explosion).

Questions

22 Calculate the momentum of the following vehicles (do not forget to define a direction).

a) A car, mass 1500 kg, travels north with a velocity of 10 m/s.

b) Concorde, mass 200 tonnes, flies south with a velocity of 500 m/s.

c) A rickshaw, occupants and driver (mass 300 kg) move north with a velocity of 3 m/s.

d) A camel and its rider, mass 1500 kg, gallop west with a velocity of 15 m/s.

23 A tennis player serves a ball, mass 0.05 kg, giving it a velocity of 40 m/s.

a) What is the ball's momentum?

b) What impulse does the racket give the ball?

c) The racket is in contact with the ball for 0.01 seconds. What is the force which the racket exerts on the ball?

d) What force does the ball exert on the racket?

24 Use the equation $F \times t$ = change of momentum to help you answer the following.

a) Why do cars have crumple zones?

b) Why do you wear a seat belt in a car?

c) When you jump down off a wall, why do you bend your legs on landing?

d) When you catch a hard ball, you move your hands backwards a little.

e) Cricketers wear pads.

A
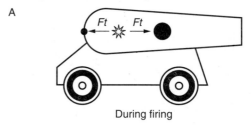
During firing

B
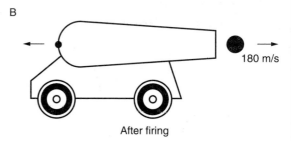
After firing

Figure 14

25 In Figure 14A a cannon ball is being fired. The ball and cannon receive equal but opposite impulses. After firing (Figure 14B), the cannon recoils. The mass of the cannon is 500 kg, the mass of the ball 2 kg, and the velocity of the ball after firing 180 m/s.

a) Calculate the momentum of the ball after firing.

b) Calculate the momentum of the cannon after firing.

c) Calculate the recoil velocity of the cannon.

d) Labelling momentum to the right as $+$ and momentum to the left as $-$, comment on the total momentum of the cannon and ball, before, during and immediately after firing.

26 For Figure 15 A–D work out the unknown velocity, v, after impact.

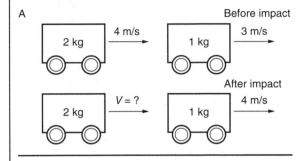

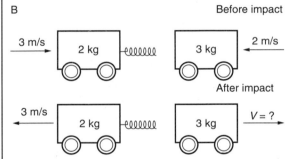

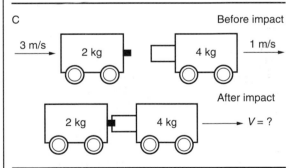

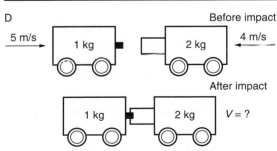

Figure 15

27 Use the principle of conservation of momentum (or Newton's third law) to explain the following:

a) A rocket can take off.

b) You can swim through water.

c) A shotgun recoils.

28 In Figure 16 an estate car slows down as it approaches heavy traffic on the motorway. Unfortunately, the lorry behind is slow to react to the situation, and runs into the back of the car. After the collision the lorry is travelling at 9 m/s.

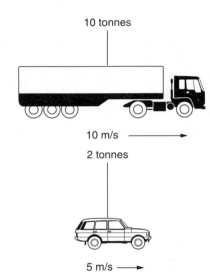

Figure 16

a) Calculate the velocity of the car after the collision.

b) Explain why head rests in the car will protect the passengers.

c) Calculate the momentum change of each driver; the lorry driver has a mass of 70 kg, the car driver 90 kg.

d) The car and lorry were in contact for 0.2 seconds. Calculate the force acting on each driver. Who is more likely to be hurt? (They were both wearing seat belts.)

29 Two cars collide head on. One is a Volvo Estate, mass 2000 kg, velocity 20 m/s travelling east; the other is a Renault Clio, mass 1000 kg, velocity 16 m/s travelling west. The cars stick together, how fast are they travelling now?

3 Earth in Space

Earth, Moon, planets, Sun, stars

▶ The Earth spins on its axis once every 24 hours. The axis of rotation points towards the Pole Star.

▶ The Moon rotates around the Earth approximately once a month (29 days).

▶ The Earth rotates around the Sun once a year.

▶ The Earth, Moon and Sun, together with eight other planets form a solar system. The other planets also rotate around the Sun. All planets are in approximately the same plane as the Earth and Sun. This is called the plane of the ecliptic.

▶ The Sun is a star which gives out light. The sky is full of other similar stars, which are huge distances away from us. Planets reflect light which the Sun gives out.

▶ Stars cluster together into galaxies. A galaxy has approximately 100 000 million stars in it. Light takes about 100 000 years to travel across a galaxy. Galaxies are separated by huge distances. Light takes 2 million years to travel from us to the Andromeda Galaxy.

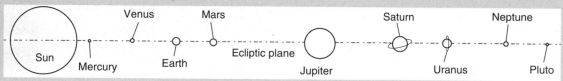

Questions

1 Explain why we have days and nights.

2 Figure 1 shows how the Earth's axis remains pointing towards the Pole Star as we orbit the Sun. Explain why we have seasons. Illustrate your answer with appropriate diagrams.

3 Tony likes to travel round the world. Recently he visited Spitzbergen, SB, Nairobi, NA, and the South Pole, S (Figure 2).

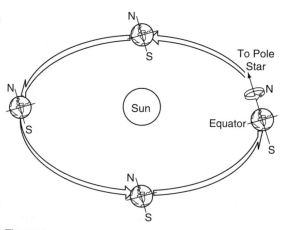

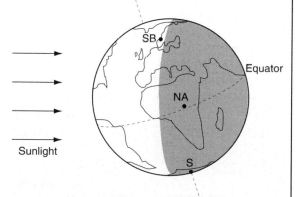

Figure 2 Earth during northern summer.

a) Explain why Tony saw the Sun at midnight in Spitzbergen, but could not see the Sun at all at the South Pole.

b) How many hours each day did Tony see the Sun in Nairobi?

c) Tony climbed Mount Batu which is just north of Nairobi. He camped at the top overnight. He claimed he saw the Pole Star. Is that possible? In which direction do you think he was looking?

d) When Tony was at the South Pole he always saw the same stars directly overhead. Explain why.

e) When Tony was in Nairobi, he saw lots of different stars overhead. Explain why.

4 Figure 3 shows the Moon's path round us each month.

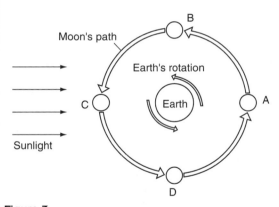

Figure 3

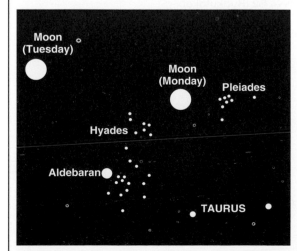

Figure 4

a) How long does it take the Moon to go from A to B?

b) Draw diagrams to show the phase of the Moon at A, B and C.

c) At what time of the day do we see (i) a full Moon, A, (ii) a half Moon, B, at their highest point in the sky?

d) Explain why the Moon appears to move past the stars each day (Figure 4).

e) Why do we never see the Moon near to the Pole Star?

5 Figure 5 shows part of the constellation of Ursa Major; the seven stars are known as the Plough. Sketch a diagram to show how they would appear to you 6 hours later. The arrow shows you the direction of rotation.

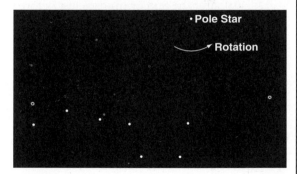

Figure 5

6 Figure 6 shows the orbits of Venus, Earth and Mars round the Sun.

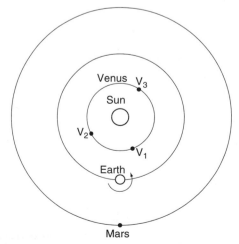

Figure 6

19

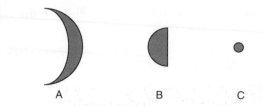

Figure 7

a) The diagrams A, B and C in Figure 7 show how Venus appears when viewed through a telescope from Earth. Match each diagram to the positions V_1, V_2, V_3 in Figure 6 (see page 19). How did this discovery help Galileo to deduce that planets went round the Sun?

b) Venus is often called the morning or the evening star; which is it in position V_1? Explain why Venus always either (i) sets just after the Sun or (ii) rises just before the Sun.

c) Use Figure 6 to explain why Mars appears to vary in brightness as it moves through the stars.

7 Voyager 1 was launched in September 1977 and passed Saturn in November 1980. It travelled about 1400 million km to Saturn.

a) Work out its average speed in millions of kilometres per year.

b) The nearest star is Alpha Centauri; this is about 4 light years away. A light year is the distance light travels in one year. Work out the distance to Alpha Centauri in millions of kilometres, given that light travels 0.3 million kilometres per second.

c) Estimate how long Voyager would take to reach Alpha Centauri travelling at the speed you calculated in part (a).

8 In early 1996 we were visited by Comet Hyakutake; Figure 8 shows its orbit as it passes Earth. Figure 9 shows how the brightness of the comet changed during its passage past Earth. The brightness of the comet changes for three reasons: it appears brighter when it is near to us; it reflects more light when closer to the Sun; when it is near the Sun, some ice melts and causes a tail to form. 'Observed magnitude' 8 is 2.5 times brighter than observed magnitude 9;

magnitude 7 is 2.5×2.5 times brighter than magnitude 9, and so on.

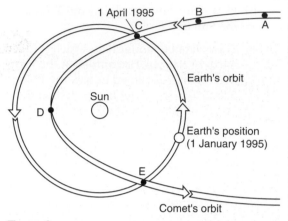

Figure 8

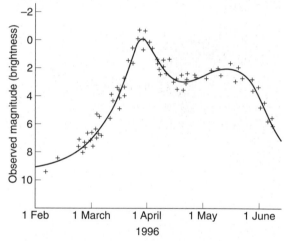

Figure 9 The observed magnitude of comet 1996 B2 (Hyakutake).

a) The graph shows two peaks in the comet's brightness. Use the information at the beginning of this question to explain why.

b) Which of the points A–E on Comet Hyakutake's orbit correspond to the two peaks in brightness?

c) What was the observed magnitude of the comet (i) in the middle of March (ii) at the end of March? By what factor did the comet increase its brightness over that period?

d) Where did the comet travel fastest in its orbit?

9 Compare the two photographs showing craters on the Moon (Figure 10A) and on Mars (Figure 10B). What are the similarities? What important difference shows that Mars has an atmosphere?

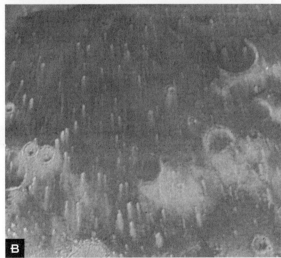

Figure 10

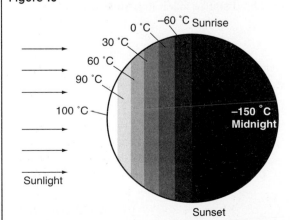

0 °C   −60 °C Sunrise
30 °C
60 °C
90 °C
100 °C
−150 °C Midnight
Sunlight
Sunset

Figure 11

10 Figure 11 shows the temperatures on the Moon's surface.

a) Which features show that the Moon has no atmosphere?

b) How does the Earth's atmosphere stabilise our temperatures?

c) Why is the temperature as low as −60 °C at sunrise on the Moon?

11 Imagine that a spacecraft could be launched at the speed of light. How long would it take to reach the following heavenly bodies? Select your answer from the list below.

(i) The Star Sirius   (v) The Sun
(ii) Jupiter   (vi) Pluto
(iii) The Andromeda   (vii) The cluster of
Galaxy   galaxies in Virgo
(iv) The far side of
the Milky Way

Possible answers:

10 000 years	9 years
2 million years	8 minutes
70 000 years	30 million years
2 seconds	1 minute
60 000 million years	5 hours
40 minutes	

12 a) Make two sketches to show the Milky Way galaxy; one sketch should shows its spiral structure and the other should show the galaxy edge on.

b) How big is the Milky Way?

c) Mark the position of the Sun in the Milky Way.

d) How many stars are there in the Milky Way?

e) How many other galaxies are there similar to the Milky Way?

f) Discuss the possibility of there being intelligent life in other galaxies.

21

13 Figure 12 shows the movement of Jupiter through the stars during 1997 and 1998. Figure 13 shows how Ptolemy (AD 120) used his theory of epicycles to explain the retrograde loop to Jupiter.

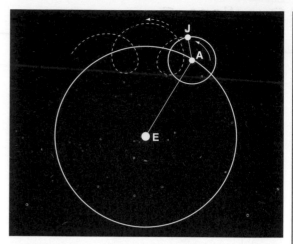

Figure 13

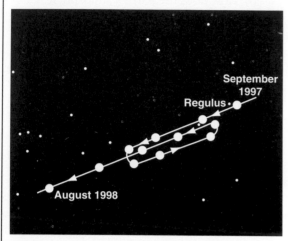

Figure 12 Jupiter's retrograde loop (Jupiter marked at one month intervals).

a) Ptolemy's theory predicts very accurately where Jupiter will be at any moment. So why don't we use it today?

b) Explain what is meant by a retrograde loop. How do we explain the apparent motion of Jupiter today? Illustrate your answer with diagrams.

Gravitation and orbits

▶ All masses in the Universe attract each other with a gravitational pull. This pull is bigger for large masses, and gets weaker as the distance between the masses gets bigger.

▶ Gravity keeps us on the Earth.

▶ Gravity acts in all directions and tends to make planets and stars sphere-shaped.

▶ The pull of gravity keeps planets in orbit round the Sun, and satellites in orbit round the Earth.

▶ The pull of gravity from the Moon and the Sun causes our tides.

▶ Newton's law of gravitation states that the force, F (in N) between two masses M_1, M_2 (in kg) whose centres are separated by a distance R (in m) is given by:

$$F = \frac{GM_1M_2}{R^2}$$

G is the universal constant of gravitation. $G = 6.7 \times 10^{-11}$ N m² kg⁻².

▶ Like any force, gravity causes objects to accelerate. Things fall close to the surface of the Earth. The Moon or other satellites also fall towards the Earth, but miss us because of their rapid sideways motion.

▶ Near the Earth things accelerate at a rate of about 10 m/s².

▶ The distance fallen in a time t is:

$$s = ut + \tfrac{1}{2}gt^2$$

s is the distance fallen, u the initial speed, and g the gravitational acceleration.

▶ When something moves in a circular path its inwards acceleration is:

$$a = \frac{v^2}{r}$$

v is its speed in m/s and r the radius of the path.

Questions

14 Each year around August 12–14 you can see a shower of meteors. These are small pieces of dust which burn up in the atmosphere and leave a bright trail. This is because the meteors are in orbit round the Sun and we cross their path each year.

   a) Why do meteors leave a bright trail in the sky?

   Large meteors are responsible for making craters on moons and sometimes the Earth. There is a large crater in the Arizona desert, which is thought to be about 20 000 years old.

   b) Most craters on the Moon have been dated as being formed 4000 million years ago. Why are craters not formed today?

   c) One side of the Moon always faces the Earth. The far side has more craters on it than the near side. Why?

   In July 1994, 20 fragments of the comet Shoemaker-Levy 9 crashed into Jupiter with speeds up to 60 km/s. The energy released by some of the largest impacts was thousands of times bigger than the energy released by the largest nuclear weapons.

   d) Why is a comet more likely to collide with Jupiter than the Earth?

15 Explain carefully why a satellite can remain in orbit round the Earth even though it uses no fuel.

16 The Earth's radius is 6400 km; a satellite is in orbit 6400 km above the Earth's surface.

   a) The mass of the satellite is 1000 kg. What is the weight of the satellite at the Earth's surface?

   b) What is the weight of the satellite while in orbit at a height of 6400 km?

   c) Draw a diagram to show the direction of the force acting on the satellite (include the Earth).

   d) While the satellite is in orbit it is accelerating, despite its speed remaining constant. How can this be?

   e) Calculate its acceleration.

17 Table 1 on page 24 gives some information about high and low tides at Plymouth in 1996.

   a) Why is only one low tide shown on June 16th?

   b) Calculate (approximately) the average interval between successive high tides. Explain why you expect this sort of value.

   c) Explain why the height of the high tides varies from day to day.

   d) When do you think it most likely that the Moon in Figure 14 was in (i) position A, (ii) position B.

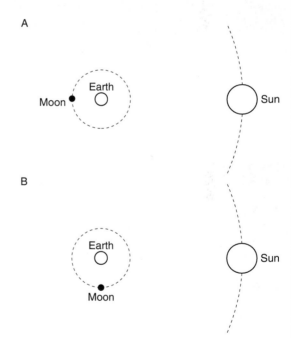

Figure 14

   e) Dartmouth lies 45 km east of Plymouth, and separate tide times are published for that area of coastline. Give two factors which cause the high and low tides to occur at different times.

18 The highest spring tides always occur in March and September. Spring tides occur when the Moon and Sun combine their tidal pull. Use Figure 15 on page 24 to help you explain this.

June

Date	Time	Tide height (m)	Date	Time	Tide height (m)
Saturday 15	0503 1125 1721 2347	5.0 1.0 5.2 1.0	Thursday 20	0205 0805 1416 2015	1.2 4.8 1.4 5.0
Sunday 16	0543 1205 1757 –	5.0 1.0 5.2 –	Friday 21	0235 0842 1445 2050	1.4 4.7 1.5 4.9
Monday 17	0026 0619 1242 1831	1.0 5.0 1.0 5.2	Saturday 22	0305 0918 1516 2126	1.5 4.6 1.7 4.8
Tuesday 18	0102 0654 1315 1905	1.0 5.0 1.1 5.2	Sunday 23	0339 0958 1555 2208	1.6 4.5 1.8 4.7
Wednesday 19	0134 0729 1346 1939	1.1 4.9 1.2 5.1	Monday 24	0426 1046 1651 2300	1.8 4.4 2.0 4.5

Table 1

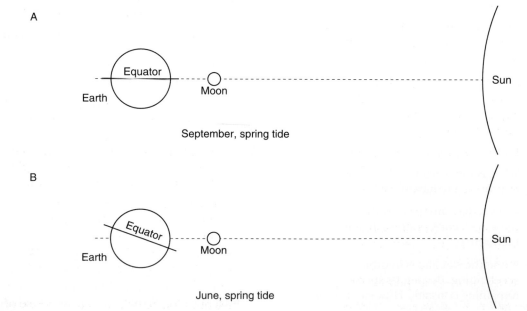

A

September, spring tide

B

June, spring tide

Figure 15

19 An astronaut has a mass of 90 kg. Explain why he feels weightless in space.

20 The Earth has a mass about 18 times that of Mercury; Earth is three times further away from the Sun than Mercury. Use Newton's law of gravitation (page 22) to compare the Sun's pull on each.

21 a) Copy Table 2. Add an extra column and work out their orbital speeds in million km per year.

Planet	Average distance from planet (million km)	Time to go round Sun (years)
Mercury	58	0.24
Venus	108	0.62
Earth	150	1.0
Mars	228	1.88
Jupiter	780	11.9
Saturn	1430	29.5
Uranus	2800	84
Neptune	4500	165
Pluto	5900	248

Table 2

b) Show that Mercury travels round the Sun with a speed ten times bigger than Pluto's.

c) Is there any pattern connecting the speed of a planet and its distance from the Sun?

d) Two satellites orbit the Earth. Metosat is in a lower orbit than Skysat; which one is travelling more quickly?

22 Metosat is in an orbit 280 km above the Earth's surface; the gravitational field strength at this height is 9 N/kg. The Earth's radius is 6400 km.

a) What is the radius of the orbit?

b) Use the equation $g = \dfrac{v^2}{r}$

to calculate the orbital speed of Metosat. (Make sure that your value of r is in metres.)

c) Work out the time period of one orbit.

The radius of the satellite's orbit is increased to three times its original value.

d) Use Newton's law of gravitation to work out the field strength at this height.

e) Work out the new orbital speed, and the new time of orbit.

23 Skysat is in a geostationary orbit round the Earth at an orbital radius of 42 300 km.

a) Explain what is meant by a geostationary orbit.

b) Why is the orbital time 24 hours?

c) Why must a geostationary orbit always be above the Equator?

d) Work out the orbital speed of Skysat.

e) Work out the gravitational field strength at this height.

24 A ball is dropped from a high cliff; $g = 10$ m/s^2.

a) Work out its speed after (i) 1 second (ii) 2 seconds (iii) 3 seconds.

b) Work out its average speed after each time.

c) Work out the distance travelled after each time.

25 A ball is thrown sideways off a cliff with a speed of 20 m/s.

a) What happens to its sideways speed during flight? (Ignore wind resistance.)

b) What happens to its downwards speed during the first 3 seconds of its fall? (You could use your answers to question 24 to help here.)

c) Draw a diagram to show the ball's path during the first 3 seconds of its fall.

26 To explain how something can remain in circular motion round a planet we might write a statement something like this.

'A satellite is pulled towards Earth by gravity, so it falls towards the Earth. However, because the satellite is moving sideways it keeps missing the Earth because the Earth's surface falls away too.'

This question helps you to make sense of this statement.

Imagine you are standing on an asteroid with a radius of 10 000 m and a gravitational field strength of 0.01 N/kg. You throw a ball sideways with a speed of 10 m/s.

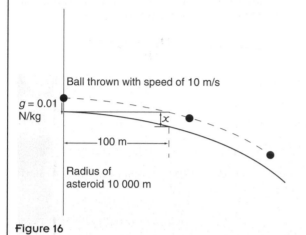

Figure 16

a) Show that the ball travels 100 m sideways in 10 seconds.

b) Assuming that the gravitational field remains in the same direction, use the equation $s = ut + \frac{1}{2}at^2$ to calculate how far the ball falls in 10 seconds (where s = distance, u = initial speed, t = time, a = acceleration). (Remember the initial downwards speed is zero.)

c) It can be shown that the asteroid's surface falls a distance of 0.5 m (x in Figure 16) over a distance of 100 m, assuming it is a perfect sphere. Comment on this value – have the ball and the asteroid's surface fallen the same distance?

d) Use the equation $g = \dfrac{v^2}{r}$ to calculate the orbital speed of the ball close to the asteroid's surface.

e) Is the statement at the beginning of this question a helpful explanation of orbital motion?

Stars

- A galaxy contains about 100 000 million stars.
- Stars produce energy by **thermonuclear fusion**; at high temperatures hydrogen nuclei (protons) fuse to form helium nuclei.
- Large stars fuse helium nuclei to make heavier elements.
- Stars which fuse hydrogen are main **sequence stars**. Stars fusing helium and larger elements are **giants** or **supergiants**.

- Stars begin their lives as large clouds of gas which collapse to form stars.
- Stars end their lives in a variety of ways. Small stars end up as **white dwarfs**. Larger stars collapse to form neutron stars or **black holes**. Very large stars explode to produce novas or **supernovas**.

Questions

27 a) What process produces energy in the Sun?

b) Which are the two most common elements found in the Sun?

c) What is the difference between a giant star and the Sun?

d) What is a white dwarf?

e) How are black holes formed?

f) What is a supernova?

28 In the Sun, energy is produced by **nuclear fusion**. Four protons fuse to form a helium nucleus and two positrons, and a lot of energy is released.

The process is described by the equation:

$4^1_1H \rightarrow {}^4_2He + 2^0_1e$.

a) A positron is a positively charged electron. How can you tell it is positively charged from the equation?

b) Why must the mass of four protons be more than that of a helium nucleus and two positrons?

c) The masses of the particles in the fusion process are given opposite, in nuclear mass units, u (u = 1.66×10^{-27} kg). Calculate the percentage mass loss in the fusion process.

mass of proton = 1.00730 u
mass of helium = 4.00260 u
mass of positron = 0.0005 u

29 Figure 17 is known as the Hertzprung–Russell diagram. It relates the brightness of a star to its surface temperature.

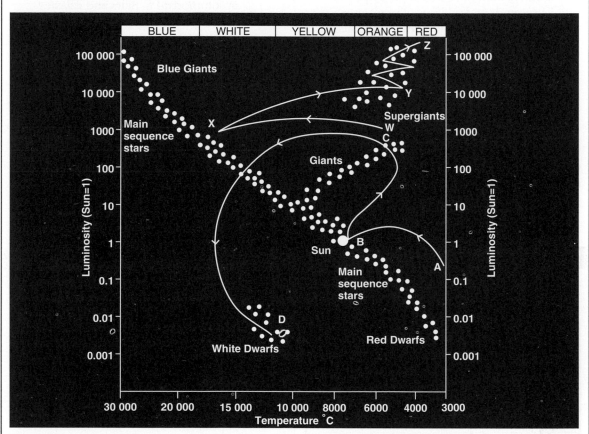

Figure 17

a) Why is there a relationship between the brightness of a star and its temperature?

b) What is the main sequence?

c) Suggest a possible relationship between the brightness of a star and its mass.

d) The lifetime of a star can be calculated using the formula $T = \dfrac{10M}{L}$.

T is the lifetime in thousands of millions of years, M is the mass relative to the Sun, and L is the star's luminosity relative to the Sun. For the Sun $M = 1$, $L = 1$.

What is the lifetime of:
  i) the Sun?
  ii) the blue giant S-Dorodus ($M = 50$, $L = 1\,000\,000$)?
  iii) a red dwarf ($M = 0.2$, $L = 0.001$)?

The line ABCD shows the evolutionary path of the Sun.

e) i) What does evolutionary path mean?
  ii) Describe what is happening at A, B, C and D.

f) The line WXYZ shows the evolutionary path of a larger star. How do you think it ends its life?

27

Cosmology

Questions ❓ ❓ ❓ ❓ ❓ ❓ ❓ ❓ ❓ ❓ ❓ ❓ ❓ ❓

30 One theory for the origin of the Universe is the **Big Bang Theory**. This suggests that the Universe originated with a giant explosion throwing mostly hydrogen and some helium outwards at great speeds. Thousands and millions of years later matter clumped together to form clusters of galaxies and stars within galaxies.

a) What force was responsible for causing galaxies and stars to form?

b) Some evidence for the Big Bang Theory is provided by the **Doppler Red Shift**.
i) Explain what is meant by a Doppler shift.
ii) Light emitted from distant galaxies has been shifted more to the red end of the spectrum than light reaching us from nearby galaxies. Why does this suggest that distant galaxies are moving away faster?

c) i) Using Table 3 plot a graph of speed against distance. Use it to explain why this data supports the Big Bang Theory.

Galaxy cluster	Distance from Earth (millions of) light years	Speed (km/s)
Virgo	70	1200
Coma Berenices	400	7000
Hercules	600	10 000
Gemini	1400	23 000
Bootes	2400	40 000

Table 3

ii) The galaxies in Pegasus are moving away at 15 000 km/s. How far away from us are they?

d) In 1960 it was discovered that the Universe was full of electromagnetic waves which appear to come from all directions. Why is this described as the echo of the Big Bang?

31 Two other theories have been put forward to explain the origin of the Universe.

I Matter is being created all the time, and as it is created the Universe expands to accommodate it. Stars and galaxies change with time, but old ones are replaced with young ones in the same way that young replace old in the human species.

II God made the Universe about 10 000 years ago. It did not evolve He just put it there. At very large distances, thousands of millions of light years, gravity becomes a repulsive force, so the galaxies are pushed apart.

a) Do you think matter could be created all the time as in theory I 'The Steady State Theory'? Is this harder to believe than the Big Bang Theory?

b) Does science rule out the possibility of God creating the Universe? If you think it does, suggest how matter might be made according to the Big Bang or Steady State Theories of creation.

c) Argue for or against the idea that gravity becomes a repulsive force at large distances.

d) Most scientists accept the Big Bang Theory. Summarise the evidence to support it.

4 Energy

Work and energy

- Work is done when a force moves an object in the *direction* of that force.
- Work is *not* done, however hard you push, if you do not move the object.
- Work is *not* done if you push at right angles to the direction in which something moves. For example when your friends give a push start to a car, and you lean on the side, you are doing nothing useful; you are not working.
- Work = force × distance
  (1 J) = (1 N) × (1 m)
  Work is measured in Joules
- Energy can be used to do work. For example, petrol has chemical energy stored in it; petrol can be used to enable a crane to lift a girder.
- Types of energy:
  - Chemical energy; stored in food or fuel.
  - Gravitational potential energy; e.g. something at the top of a hill has stored energy.
  - Kinetic energy; this is the name given to the energy associated with a moving object.
  - Heat energy; atoms in a hot object move quickly and randomly. In cold objects they move more slowly.
  - Electrical energy.
  - Strain energy; a stretched rubber band, or bent stick has strain energy.
  - Sound energy; a plucked guitar string makes the air vibrate backwards and forwards.
  - Nuclear energy; the nucleus of an atom has energy stored in it.
  - Light energy; this is given out by hot objects (lamps and flames).
- The principle of Conservation of Energy tells us that energy cannot be created or destroyed. Energy can be turned from one form into another.

Questions

1 In the following cases explain *carefully* the energy changes or transfers which occur. Do not first write something like 'potential to kinetic', be specific; where is the energy? Is the energy given to another object?

  a) You pluck a guitar string, and your friend hears a sound.

  b) You fire a marble with a catapult, and accidentally break a window.

  c) You throw a ball vertically upwards.

  d) You kick a football along the ground, it comes to a halt.

  e) Energy is transferred from the Sun, to warm you up while sunbathing.

  f) You accelerate a car, then bring it to rest using the brakes.

  g) A firework rocket takes off, explodes and falls back to the ground.

2 Figure 1 shows the path of a comet going round the Sun. The comet has the same *total* energy at any point along its path.

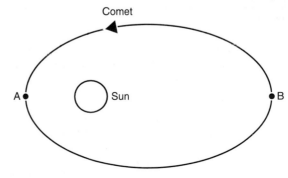

Figure 1

29

a) Explain why the comet's potential energy is greatest at B, and least at A.

b) Where will the comet be travelling fastest? Explain your answer.

3 Figure 2 shows a section of track near a railway station. The track at the station is slightly higher than the rest of the track. What advantage does this give? Explain your answer in terms of energy changes.

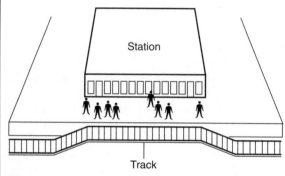

Figure 2

4 Figure 3 shows the path of a cannon ball.

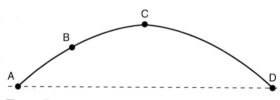

Figure 3

a) Where is it travelling most slowly? Explain your answer.

b) Table 1 shows the potential and kinetic energies of the ball in various positions. Copy and complete the table. (You can ignore any wind resistance.)

Position	Potential energy (J)	Kinetic energy (J)
A	0	1000
B	200	
C		600
D		

Table 1

5 Name devices that can be used to change:

a) sound energy to electrical energy

b) heat energy to kinetic energy

c) electrical energy to kinetic energy

d) kinetic energy to electrical energy

6 Which of the following forces are doing work?

a) A magnetic force holding a magnet onto a steel door.

b) A force driving a car forward.

c) A weight-lifter holding a weight stationary.

d) A paper weight holding down a pile of paper.

e) A crane applying a force to lift a load.

f) The pull of gravity holding a satellite in a circular orbit around the Earth.

7 A box has a weight of 250 N. It is pulled 10 m along the ground using a spring balance which reads 50 N. The box is then lifted through a height of 2 m. How much work is done in total?

8 Three physics students decide to compare the force of wind resistance on their cars. They decide to carry out a fair test to see how far each car can travel, at a constant speed of 70 km per hour, using only 5 litres of petrol. Table 2 shows their results.

Car	Distance travelled (km)
Renault Clio	75
Astra 1.3 l	70
Volvo 440	50

Table 2

a) Which car do you think is the most streamlined?

b) Compare the resistive forces on the Renault and Volvo, when they travel at 70 km per hour.

c) Their teacher tells them it is not really a fair test. What factors have they forgotten?

Calculating energy

It is often useful to work out how much energy there is in a system. Here are some formulae.

▶ **Gravitational potential energy** = mgh
  m = mass of body
  g = gravitational field strength (10 N/kg on Earth)
  h = height of body above the ground

▶ **Kinetic energy** = $\frac{1}{2}mv^2$
  m = mass of body
  v = the speed of the body

▶ **Strain energy** = average force × distance stretched.
  The average force is usually *half* the final force for a stretched spring.

▶ **Heat energy gained** = mass × specific heat capacity × temperature rise.

▶ **Power** is defined as **work** done per second.

So Power = $\dfrac{\text{work}}{\text{time}}$

The unit of power is $\dfrac{\text{joule (J)}}{\text{second}}$ or watt (W).

Questions ❓❓❓❓❓❓❓❓❓❓❓❓❓❓❓

9 You can see the profile of a fairground ride in Figure 4. A car leaves point A and arrives later at point F. The mass of the car, including occupants, is 200 kg.

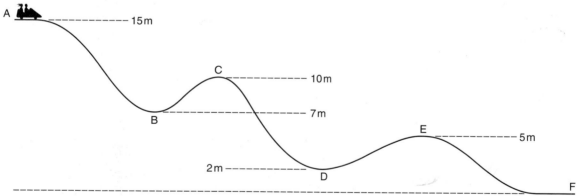

Figure 4

a) Calculate the car's potential energy at each of the points A to F.

b) Now calculate the car's speed at each of the points B to F. Assume its speed was very small at A.

10 A bullet is fired vertically upwards from a gun at 100 m/s. What is the maximum height it can reach?

11 A trolley is pushed towards slope A in Figure 5, and its midpoint (x) comes to a halt 20 cm up the slope.

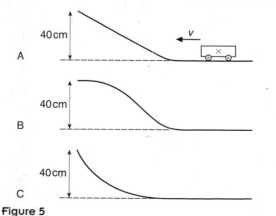

Figure 5

31

a) How far up the slopes B and C will the trolley go, if it is pushed at the same starting speed?

b) Does the trolley stop most quickly in case A, B or C? Explain your answer.

12 A bullet of mass 0.05 kg is fired at a speed of 200 m/s.

a) Calculate the bullet's kinetic energy.

b) The bullet hits a tree and penetrates to a depth of 10 cm. Calculate the average force acting to slow it down.

c) Calculate the temperature rise of the bullet, assuming all its kinetic energy turns into heat energy. (The specific heat capacity of the bullet is 400 J/kg °C.)

d) Explain why the bullet will not warm up as much as you have calculated.

13 You have just taken over as the manager of a bungee jumping company. You want to give people a thrill, without plunging them into the river below! Work through the following calculation to check on the jump's safety.

a) Calculate the potential energy which Angus (mass = 80 kg) loses after falling (i) 10 m, (ii) 30 m. Check your answers agree with Figure 6B.

b) Use the formula: strain energy = average force × extension, to estimate the tension in the rope, when its length is 30 m.

c) Use the graph to predict when Angus comes to a halt.

d) Mike, mass 100 kg, and Zoe, mass 50 kg, want to jump too.
i) Use the graph to show that Mike will land in the river.
ii) Predict how far Zoe falls.

e) What can you do to make the jump safe for Mike?

f) What problems would you face if the rope is (i) too stiff (ii) too floppy?

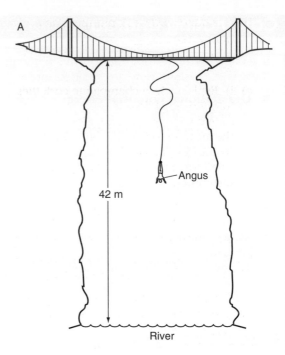

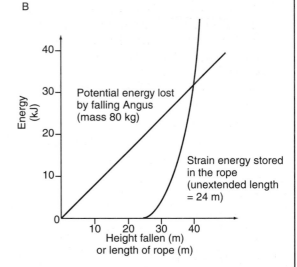

Figure 6

14 When we talk about pressure, we usually think of the equation $P = \dfrac{F}{A}$, and express pressure in units of N/m². It can also be useful to think of pressure as **energy** per unit volume, and to use units of J/m³.

a) Explain why units of N/m² and J/m³ are the same.

b) It is quite hard work pumping up a bicycle tyre. Explain why there is potential energy stored in an inflated tyre.

c) i) Explain why a champagne cork flies into the air when released.
ii) A cork, mass 0.02 kg, flies 10 m into the air when released from a 70 cl (0.0007 m^3) bottle. Estimate the excess pressure in the bottle, stating any assumptions you make.

15 a) A car, mass 1200 kg, slows from 30 m/s to 20 m/s. Calculate the change in its kinetic energy.

b) The car slowed over a distance of 40 m, calculate the average braking force.

16 People often think that the most important thing about a car is its engine size or design. However, the brakes are the most important feature. When you learn to drive you need to be able to judge your stopping distance. This is made up of two parts. Your **thinking** distance where you keep travelling at your original speed while you react to a problem (a slow reaction time would be 0.7 seconds). Then your **braking** distance where the brakes act to remove the car's kinetic energy.

a) Assume your reaction time is 0.7 seconds. Copy Table 3 and fill in the gaps for thinking distance.

Speed (m/s)	10	20	30	40
Thinking distance (m)		14		
Braking distance (m)	10		90	
Total distance (m)				188

Table 3

b) Suppose you and your car have a mass of 1200 kg. When the brakes are applied carefully a force of 6000 N is applied to the wheels.
i) Use the idea that the brakes do work to remove kinetic energy, to show that the car's braking distance, at an initial speed of 10 m/s, is 10 m.
ii) Complete the rest of the table.

c) Three friends with their luggage get into the car to increase the total mass to 1500 kg. What difference does this make to your total stopping distance?

d) When you travel at 30 m/s on the motorway in clear visibility, what do you think is a safe distance between you and the car in front?

e) On a foggy day your visibility is only 40 m. Show that your maximum safe speed is about 17 m/s.

f) What difference does it make to your stopping distance if you are travelling downhill. Explain your answer in terms of energy changes.

17 Artur is a shire horse used for ploughing fields. He pulls a ploughshare which is 2.5 m across, at a steady speed of 1.2 m/s applying a force of 800 N. He sets out to plough a field of area 2 hectares (200 m × 100 m).

a) How far does Artur walk to plough the field?

b) How much work has he done in ploughing the field?

c) How long did Artur take to plough the field?

d) Calculate the *useful* power Artur developed during ploughing. Express your answer in W and horsepower. (1 horsepower = 746 W.)

18 How much power is developed in the following cases?

a) A weight-lifter lifts 200 kg through 2 m in 3 seconds.

b) A high jumper, mass 70 kg, lifts his centre of gravity through 1.2 m. During take-off his leg is in contact with the ground for 0.3 seconds.

c) A high-speed train, travelling at a constant speed of 40 m/s, working against resistive forces of 20 kN.

Machines and efficiency

▶ Machines are devices which can multiply forces for us. They allow us to exert a small force which then exerts a large force somewhere else. *Note:* machines **do not** multiply energy for us.

▶ **Mechanical advantage** $= \dfrac{\text{load}}{\text{effort}}$ (of a machine)

▶ **Efficiency** $= \dfrac{\text{useful work out}}{\text{work put in}}$

▶ **Velocity ratio** $= \dfrac{\text{distance moved by effort}}{\text{distance moved by load}}$

Questions

19 Figure 7 shows a lever being used to lift a rock.

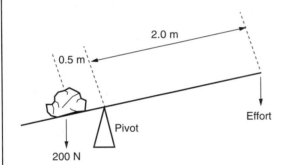

Figure 7

a) What effort force must be applied to lift the rock?

b) If the rock is lifted 0.25 m, how much work has been done on it?

c) How much work will the effort force have done to lift the load?

20 An electric winch is used to pull a coal truck up an inclined plane (Figure 8).

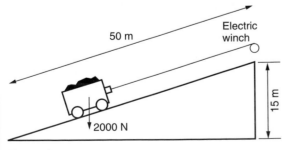

Figure 8

a) How much useful work is done in lifting the load through 15 m?

The winch uses a 6 kW electrical supply, and pulls the truck up the slope at a rate of 5 m/s.

b) How long does it take to pull the truck up the slope?

c) How much work is done by the winch?

d) Calculate the efficiency of the machine. Where do you think energy losses occur?

21 For each of the following explain where the effort is applied and what the load is.

a) spanner turning a nut

b) car jack lifting a car

c) vice holding a block

d) corkscrew in a cork

22 Pete and Wesley are two muscle men. Stephen is not as strong, but he has devised a machine to beat Pete and Wesley in a trial of strength (Figure 9). Explain how Stephen can win.

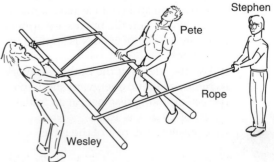

Figure 9

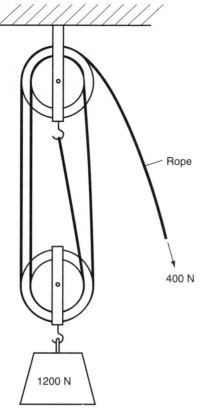

Rope

400 N

1200 N

Figure 10

23 Look at the pulley system in Figure 10. Calculate:

a) its mechanical advantage

b) velocity ratio

c) the work done on the load when it is lifted 0.5 m

d) the work done by the *effort* when the load is lifted 0.5 m

e) the efficiency of this pulley system.

Energy resources

Question ❓ ❓ ❓ ❓ ❓ ❓ ❓ ❓ ❓ ❓ ❓ ❓ ❓ ❓ ❓

24 Explain why all of the Earth's energy comes originally from the Sun.

25 Explain how fossil fuels were formed.

26 a) What is a renewable energy source; give three examples.

b) What is a non-renewable energy source; give three examples.

27 Explain in detail the energy changes which occur in a power station to change the chemical energy, stored in coal, into electrical energy. Use diagrams where appropriate.

28 Give and explain two advantages and two disadvantages of using wind power.

29 At Vasterfjall in Sweden it is proposed to build a small hydroelectric power station to provide electricity for the local community, population 20 000. Figure 11 (see page 36) shows the average power needed by the town over a year, and the average flow rate of water down the mountain. At the site the water flows at a speed of about 25 m/s. It is only possible to divert about 20% of the stream for power generation purposes, and the turbogenerators are about 40% efficient.

a) Explain why the demand for power varies over the year.

b) Explain why the water flow varies over the year.

35

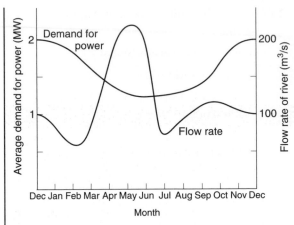

Figure 11

c) Calculate the amount of kinetic energy in (i) 1 kg (ii) 1 m³ of falling water. (Density of water = 1000 kg/m³.)

d) Use the graph and the information at the beginning of this question to calculate the (i) maximum and (ii) minimum power available from the station.

e) Comment on whether this station can reliably supply electricity to the community.
The cost of the power station will be 28 million Swedish krone (kr). The interest will have to be repaid at a rate of 14% per annum, and running costs per year will be 1.5 million krone. At the moment the people of Vasterfjall pay Swedish Hydro-Electric 0.5 kr per kWh.

f) Estimate the number of kWh used annually by the Vasterfjall community.

g) Work out the cost of home-produced electricity per kWh, and comment on the economic feasibility of the station.

5 Matter

Kinetic theory

▶ Matter is made up of moving particles (e.g. atoms and molecules). If the temperature of a substance is increased, its particles move about faster.
▶ The particles of a solid vibrate about fixed positions.
▶ The particles of a gas are free to move in all directions.
▶ The particles of a liquid are free to move over each other, but are still held closely together.

▶ The pressure exerted by the particles of a gas in a container can be increased by:
i) adding more gas particles (this increases the number of collisions per second);
ii) reducing the volume of the container (this also increases the number of collisions per second);
iii) increasing the temperature (this increases the particles' speed and therefore the number of collisions per second).

Questions

1 a) Name the three states of matter.

b) Suppose a substance changes from one state to another without decomposing. In which state of matter would you expect the substance to be (i) most dense, (ii) least dense, (iii) most compressible? Give reasons for your answers.

c) There are exceptions to these generalisations, e.g. water. Water behaves differently because of 'hydrogen bonding'. In what way does the behaviour of water differ?

d) In which of the three states of matter would you expect the particles of a substance to be:
i) most ordered?
ii) least ordered?
iii) moving around freely in all directions?
iv) vibrating to and fro about fixed positions?

e) The ability of atoms and molecules to attract each other does not vanish when a solid substance becomes a gas. Explain why the molecules of the substance in the gaseous state are no longer held together, as they are in the solid state.

2 a) How does increasing the temperature of a solid substance affect the way its atoms or molecules vibrate?

b) Figure 1 represents some translating atoms, or molecules, of a substance in the gaseous state, at two different temperatures. In which diagram is the gas (i) hottest, (ii) coldest? How can you tell?

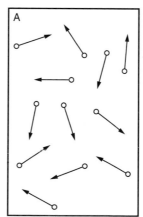
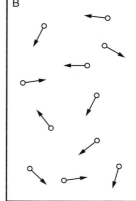

Figure 1

c) Explain the terms *vibrating* and *translating*. Explain why we should use the word *average* when describing molecular motion.

37

3 a) In order to liquefy a gaseous substance you could simply cool it down. What does cooling down do to the molecules of the gas, that causes it to become a liquid?

b) If the temperature of a gaseous substance is close to its boiling point, you can liquefy the gas by compressing it. A gas which can be liquefied by pressure alone is called a *vapour*. How does compressing a vapour cause it to become a liquid?

c) If you were to compress a vapour to the liquid state and then release the pressure, the liquid would start to evaporate. Explain, using a diagram, why some molecules leave the liquid immediately, while others do not.

4 Figure 2 demonstrates an experiment which provides evidence of molecular motion. A small trace of smoke is drawn into a transparent container of air. The container is lit from the side and its contents are viewed using a low powered microscope. The smoke particles can be seen to move in a haphazard manner. This effect is called **Brownian motion**.

a) Why don't the smoke particles fall to the bottom of the container?

b) Using arrows, sketch the magnified motion of a single smoke particle.

c) Air molecules are much smaller than smoke particles and cannot be seen through the microscope. Explain how this demonstration provides evidence of their existence, and of their motion.

5 Explain the following in terms of 'molecules in motion'.

a) When bromine is introduced into a vessel containing air, the bromine spreads out very slowly. However, if the vessel has been evacuated first, it fills with bromine very quickly.

b) At room temperature air molecules and vapour molecules move about at very high speeds. Why do smells (vapour molecules) travel across a room very slowly?

c) An iron bar expands when it is heated.

d) Air trapped in a corked bottle left in strong sunlight, results in the cork blowing out.

e) The effect described in part (d) is far more dramatic if a little wine is left in the bottle.

f) Clothes hung on a line to dry, dry more quickly in a breeze, than in still air.

g) If some ether is placed in a beaker and allowed to evaporate, the ether remaining in the beaker *cools*.

6 The piston for the bicycle pump in Figure 3 is pushed in slowly until the air pressure inside the pump *trebles*. The air in the pump remains at a constant temperature of 20 °C.

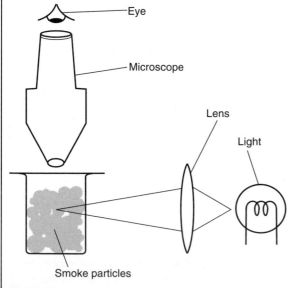

Figure 2

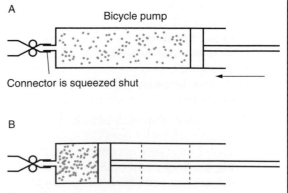

Figure 3

a) Describe the motion of the air molecules in the pump in Figure 3.

b) Explain in terms of molecular motion why the pressure in B should be three times greater than in A.

c) Moving the piston in very slowly ensures that the enclosed air remains at the same temperature. Why? What does this tell you about the average speed of the molecules before and after compression?

d) What would have happened if the piston had been pushed in quickly?

e) Explain in terms of molecular motion, why heating the enclosed air increases the pressure it exerts.

The gas laws

In the following equations P = pressure, V = volume, and T = temperature in degrees kelvin (K).

▶ *Boyle's law:* $P \times V$ = constant (provided the temperature and mass of gas do not change).

▶ *Charles' law:* $P \propto T$ (provided the volume and mass of gas do not change).

▶ *The pressure law:* $V \propto T$ (provided the pressure and mass of gas do not change).

▶ The gas laws can be combined into the

equation: $\dfrac{PV}{T}$ = constant where T is in

degrees kelvin (K).

▶ For two different pressures, volumes and

temperatures: $\dfrac{P_1 V_1}{T_1} = \dfrac{P_2 V_2}{T_2}$

▶ *Absolute zero* (0 K) is the temperature at which the particles in a gas would stop moving (and exert zero pressure), if the gas did not liquefy.

▶ Temperature (in K) = temperature (in °C) + 273

▶ 0 K = −273 °C

▶ 0 °C = 273 K

Questions ❓ ❓ ❓ ❓ ❓ ❓ ❓ ❓ ❓ ❓ ❓ ❓ ❓ ❓ ❓

7 The apparatus in Figure 4 (see page 40) is used to investigate how the gas pressure (in this case air) depends on the volume it occupies. The air is contained in a thick walled glass tube; its volume can be reduced by forcing oil up into the tube. The pressure reading on the gauge gives the pressure above the oil in the reservoir, which is assumed to be equal to the pressure of the trapped air. The temperature of the trapped air does not change.

a) Draw a diagram to show the construction of a Bourdon pressure gauge and explain how it works.

b) The reading on the pressure gauge will be very slightly greater than the pressure of the trapped air: (i) explain why (ii) explain why this does not matter.

c) What happens to the pressure of the trapped air if the volume is halved?

d) Copy and complete Table 1 (see page 40) by entering the values of $P \times V$ in the third row.

e) Describe the relationship between the volume and the pressure of a fixed mass of gas, at constant temperature.

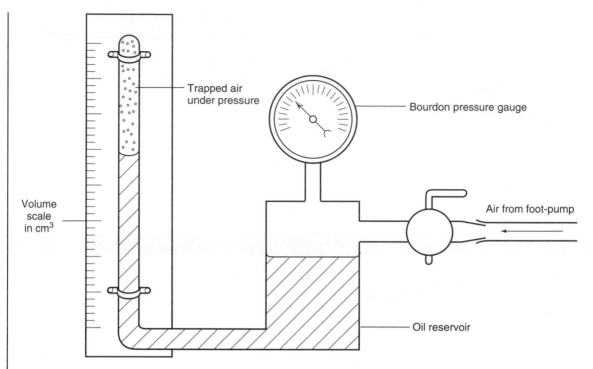

Figure 4

Volume of trapped air (in cm³)	40.0	33.3	28.6	25.0	22.2	20.0
Pressure reading (in kN/m²)	100	120	140	160	180	200
P × V						

Table 1

8 Referring to the experiment described in question 7 and Table 1:

a) What volume would you expect the trapped air to occupy, when its pressure is (i) 300 kN/m², (ii) 50 kN/m²?

b) What pressure would you expect the trapped air to exert when its volume is (i) 16 cm³, (ii) 60 cm³?

c) Plot a graph of P (y-axis) against V (x-axis).

d) Why is it difficult to use the graph to check your answers to parts (a) and (b)?

e) Use a calculator to work out values of $\dfrac{1}{V}$. Plot a graph of P against $\dfrac{1}{V}$. Why is this graph more useful than the graph in part (c)? Use the new graph to check your answers to parts (a) and (b).

f) Questions 7 and 8 are about Boyle's law. State Boyle's law.

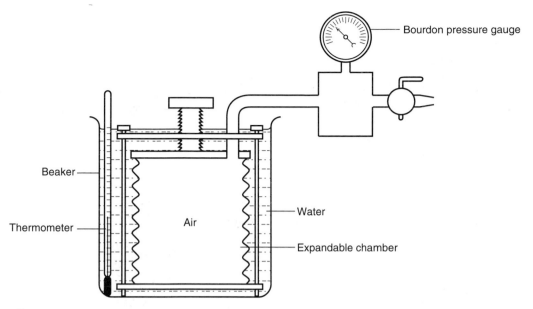

Bourdon pressure gauge

Beaker

Water

Thermometer

Air

Expandable chamber

Figure 5

9 Figure 5 shows a piece of apparatus used to investigate how gas pressure varies with temperature, at constant volume. Table 2 shows a set of results.

Temperature (in °C)	26	50	65	80	100
Pressure reading (in kN/m²)	102	110	115	120	127

Table 2

a) Plot a graph of pressure, P (y-axis), against temperature, T, in °C (x-axis). Use it to find the pressure of the enclosed gas at 70 °C.

b) The graph enables you to make predictions about the pressure outside the range of values plotted. How?

c) If the gas pressure continued to vary in the way suggested by the graph, what pressure would you expect at (i) 200 °C, (ii) 0 °C, (iii) −200 °C.

d) Is it correct to say that the pressure is proportional to temperature? Why?

e) Where does the line cross the temperature axis (it should be between −270 and −280 °C). What will the gas pressure be at this temperature?

10 The apparatus in Figure 5 can also be used to investigate how the volume of a gas varies with temperature, at constant pressure.

Temperature (in °C)	0	23	45	68	91
Volume (in cm³)	600	650	700	750	800

Table 3

a) Describe how you would carry out this experiment.

b) Plot a graph of volume, V (y-axis), against temperature, T, in °C (x-axis) using Table 3.

c) If the volume of the gas continued to vary in the way suggested by the graph, what volume would you expect at (i) 200 °C, (ii) 0 °C, (iii) −200 °C?

d) Find where the line cuts the temperature axis (it should be between −270 and −280 °C). What will the volume of the gas be at this temperature?

11 Graphs of pressure (or volume) against temperature for gases have one thing in common – they cut the temperature axis at the same place, $-273\,°C$. This implies that the volume (or pressure) of a gas tends to zero at $-273\,°C$, if the gas does not liquefy. Such a gas is called an **ideal gas**. The **Kelvin temperature scale** starts from $-273\,°C$ instead of $0\,°C$.

a) Explain the meaning of the term 'ideal'.

b) What would happen to the molecular motion of an ideal gas at $-273\,°C$?

c) If temperature is a measure of molecular motion, explain why $-273\,°C$ is referred to as 'absolute zero'.

d) Convert the following temperatures to kelvin (K):
(i) $0\,°C$; (ii) $100\,°C$; (iii) $-100\,°C$.

e) Convert the following temperatures to Celsius (°C):
(i) 273 K; (ii) 300 K; (iii) 200 K.

12 We can make predictions about the pressures, volumes and temperatures of gases, if we assume they behave like ideal gases. Most gases behave like this, so long as they are nowhere near their liquefaction point nor at very high pressure. The properties of these gases is summarised by the equation: $\dfrac{PV}{T} = $ constant. For two different situations we can equate them as:

$$\frac{P_1 V_1}{T_1} = \frac{P_2 V_2}{T_2}.$$

a) Why does this equation represent Boyle's law, if temperature is constant?

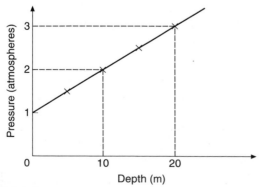

b) A fish releases a bubble from a depth of 20 m below the surface of a lake. Figure 6 shows how pressure increases with depth. How many times larger will the bubble be at the surface? (Assume temperature is constant.)

c) The pressure in an inflated car tyre at $27\,°C$ is 250 kPa. What will the pressure be at $57\,°C$? (Assume constant volume.)

d) On a very warm day ($27\,°C$) a kilogram of atmospheric air occupies a volume of about $0.8\ m^3$. What volume will a kilogram of atmospheric air occupy on a very cold day ($-3\,°C$)? (Assume constant pressure.)

13 The temperature of the inert gas in a mains light bulb, under operating conditions, is $327\,°C$. The mass of gas inside the bulb is chosen so that the pressure inside the light bulb is equal to the atmospheric pressure outside (100 kPa).

a) Convert $327\,°C$ to kelvin.

b) Calculate the pressure of the inert gas inside the bulb when it is *not operating*. Assume that room temperature is $17\,°C$.

c) If you drop the bulb at room temperature, will it implode or explode? Why?

d) Suppose the *same mass* of gas is placed in a bulb which has *twice the volume*.

i) What will the pressure of the gas be at $327\,°C$?
ii) At what temperature will the pressure of the gas inside the larger bulb equal the pressure outside (120 kPa)?

Figure 6

6 Heat

Specific heat

Work = force × distance

Circumference of circle = 2π × radius

$$\text{Power} = \frac{\text{energy}}{\text{time}}$$

- The heat content of a body, sometimes called its internal or thermal energy, is the *total* mechanical energy associated with the *disordered* motion of its particles.
- Temperature is a measure of 'hotness' and depends on the *average* kinetic energy of individual particles.
- The heat capacity of a body is the amount of heat required to raise its temperature by 1 °C.
- The specific heat capacity of a substance is the amount of heat required to raise the temperature of 1 kg of the substance by 1 °C.

- The units of heat capacity are J/°C.
- The units of specific heat capacity are J/°C per kg (usually written as J/kg °C).

When two bodies exchange heat with each other (e.g. if you poured hot soup into a cold bowl), the heat exchange is summarised by the statement:

Heat energy *lost* by hot body = heat energy *gained* by cold body.

- Heat *taken in* by a body (J) = specific heat capacity (J/°C kg) × mass (kg) × temperature *rise* (°C).
- Heat *given out* by a body (J) = specific heat capacity (J/°C kg) × mass (kg) × temperature *drop* (°C).
- Heat given out by a heater (J) = power of heater (J/s) × time (s).

Questions

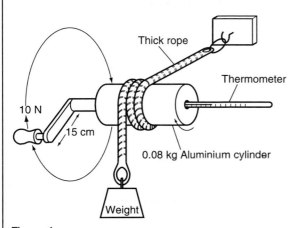

Figure 1

1 The apparatus in Figure 1 can be used to show how mechanical work produces heat. You have to apply force to the handle to oppose the frictional force between the rope and the cylinder. This force can be measured by attaching a spring balance to the handle. Turning the handle raises the temperature of the aluminium cylinder. Table 1 shows the results from one experiment.

Force on handle	= 10 N
Radius of handle	= 15 cm
Number of turns	= 30
Mass of aluminium cylinder	= 0.08 kg
Temperature of cylinder at start	= 21 °C
Temperature of cylinder after 30 turns	= 25 °C

Table 1

43

a) Calculate the work done to rotate the handle through one complete circle.

b) Calculate the work done for 30 turns of the handle.

c) What is the temperature rise of the cylinder after 30 turns?

d) Calculate the work done per degree rise in temperature.

e) Calculate the work required to raise the temperature of 1 kg of aluminium by 1 °C.

f) If the work done is equal to the heat energy gained by the cylinder, how much heat energy is required to raise 1 kg of aluminium by 1 °C (i.e. the specific heat capacity)?

2 To raise the temperature of 1 kg of aluminium by 1 °C you need 883 J of energy. An electrical heater is used to supply energy to a 1 kg block of aluminium.

a) Plot a graph of temperature (y-axis) against time (x-axis) using Table 2.

b) Why did the thermometer reading not increase immediately the heater was switched on?

c) Use your graph to find out how long it took for the temperature to increase from 23 °C to 27 °C.

d) Calculate the heat energy required for this temperature rise.

e) Calculate the power of the heater.

3 Samantha and Tim decide to carry out an experiment to measure solar energy. They borrow a parabolic reflector from school and use it to focus radiation from the Sun onto a copper block (Figure 2). The effective area of the reflector is 1 m², the mass of copper is 5 kg and its specific heat capacity is 400 J/kg °C. The temperature of the block increases by 18 °C in 1 minute.

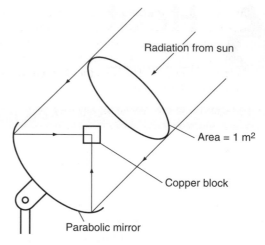

Radiation from sun

Area = 1 m²

Copper block

Parabolic mirror

Figure 2

Data:	Distance of Sun to Earth $= 1.5 \times 10^{11}$ m
Assume:	The energy from the Sun is spread out in all directions. The energy falling on the reflector is equal to the energy falling on 1 m² of the surface of a sphere of radius 1.5×10^{11} m
Formula:	The surface area of a sphere $= 4\pi r^2$ (r = the radius of the sphere)

Table 3

a) Calculate the heat energy transferred to the block in 1 minute.

b) Calculate the energy falling on the reflector each second.

c) What have you assumed in answering these questions?

d) If the atmosphere absorbs about half of the solar energy passing through it, calculate the energy per second falling on the reflector if there were no atmosphere.

e) Use part (d) and Table 3 to estimate the total energy per second emitted from the Sun.

Time (s)	0	60	120	180	240	300	360
Temperature (°C)	20	20	21	23	25	27	29

44 | Table 2

4 In the shower unit in Michael's house, cold water enters at 20 °C, flows past a heater and warms to 40 °C. The hot water emerges from the shower head at the rate of 1 kg every 10 seconds. The specific heat capacity of water is 4200 J/kg °C.

a) Calculate the rate at which heat energy transfers to the water.

b) Assuming there is no heat loss, what is the power output of the heater?

c) Without altering the heater's power, what other change could Michael make to obtain hotter water?

5 Jane wishes to measure the temperature of the water from the hot tap in her bathroom which she thinks is about 60 °C. The only thermometer in the house is a clinical one, which reads up to 40 °C. She decides to mix equal quantities of hot and cold water and to measure the temperature of the mixture. The temperature of the cold water is 18 °C and the mixture 36 °C. Jane assumes that the energy lost from the hot water is equal to the energy gained by the cold water.

a) Calculate the temperature of the hot water.

b) What temperature will the mixture be if the proportions are 1 kg of hot water at 60 °C and 2 kg of cold water at 20 °C?

6 Use Table 4 to answer the following:

Substance	Specific heat capacity (J/kg °C)
water	4200
copper	380
lead	130

Table 4

a) How much heat energy is required to raise the temperature of 2 kg of:
   i) water from 20 °C to 100 °C?
   ii) copper from 20 °C to 100 °C?

b) How much heat energy is removed to cool down 2 kg of:
   i) water from 100 °C to 20 °C?
   ii) copper from 100 °C to 20 °C?

c) How much heat must be extracted to cool down 3 kg of lead from 20 °C to -10 °C?

d) Calculate the temperature rise if 2×10^4 J is transferred to 3 kg of copper. If the starting temperature of the copper is 20 °C, what is its final temperature?

e) Calculate the mass of water, which when cooled from 80 °C to 30 °C releases 6×10^5 J.

f) What extra information do you need to calculate the heat energy released by 2 kg water as it cools down from (say) 20 °C to -10 °C?

7 An electric night-time storage heater (Figure 3) uses cheap rate electricity to heat up a 40 kg block of concrete. The heater is thermostatically controlled. The concrete releases the stored heat energy during the day to heat a room. Use Table 5 to answer the following:

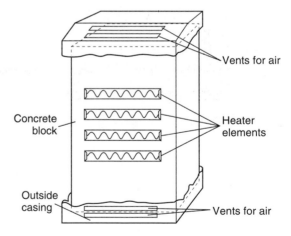

Figure 3

Volume of air in room	=	46 m³
Power provided by heating elements	=	800 W
Specific heat capacity of concrete	=	840 J/kg °C
Specific heat capacity of air	=	120 J/kg °C
Density of air	=	1 kg/m³

Table 5

a) Why do electricity generating boards make electrical power cheaper at night-time?

b) What does 'thermostatically controlled' mean?

c) If the heater elements supply energy for 2 hours during the night, calculate the heat energy given to the concrete block?

d) Suppose only half the heat energy given to the concrete during the night is retained. What would be the temperature rise of the concrete block?

e) During the first hour of the day the concrete block cools by 20 °C. Calculate the heat energy transferred to the room during this time.

f) Calculate the temperature rise of the air in the room during the first hour of the day.

g) The air temperature after 1 hour is nowhere near the temperature calculated in part (f). Explain why.

Latent heat

- When a pure substance melts or boils, it takes in heat energy.
- When a pure substance solidifies or condenses, it gives out heat energy.
- When a pure substance is melting, or boiling, its temperature does not change because energy is used to break bonds, rather than increasing the movement of particles.
- Specific latent heat of fusion is the amount of heat required to melt 1 kg of a substance.

- Specific latent heat of vaporisation is the amount of heat required to vaporise 1 kg of a substance.
- Heat taken in when melting (J) = specific latent heat of fusion (J/kg) × mass melted (kg).
- Heat taken in when vaporising (J) = specific latent heat of vaporisation (J/kg) × mass vaporised (kg).
- Similar equations can be used to calculate the heat *given out* when a substance solidifies or condenses.

Questions

8 Hank and Liza use the apparatus shown in Figure 4 to determine the specific latent heat of vaporisation of water. They heat the water from room temperature (20 °C) to its boiling point (100 °C), and then boil it steadily. A graph is plotted of the balance reading against time (Figure 5).

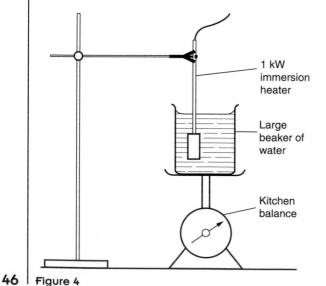

Figure 4

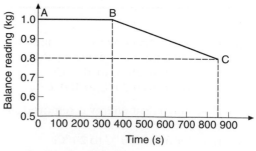

Figure 5

a) Describe what is happening to the water in (i) region AB, (ii) region BC of the graph.

b) Draw a temperature–time graph for the water in the beaker for region ABC.

c) Calculate the heat energy released from the heater during boiling.

d) Assuming there is no heat loss to the surroundings, calculate a value for the specific latent heat of vaporisation of the water.

e) There are bound to be heat losses, so your answer to part (d) will be inaccurate. Will it be too large or too small? Why?

f) Liza suggests using a 2 kW heater. Hank says this will give an even worse result. Is Hank right? Why?

g) Liza suggests doing the experiment twice, first with the 1 kW heater, and then with a 2 kW heater. How is it possible to combine the results of both experiments to get a more accurate result?

9 One of the diagrams in Figure 6 represents the heat exchange unit of a refrigerator.

a) In which direction is heat energy being transferred in Figure 6A, from P to X or X to P?

b) In which direction is heat energy being transferred in Figure 6B?

c) Which represents the heat exchange unit in a refrigerator?

d) Explain how heat exchange can occur, even if the temperature of the substance passing through the exchanger does not change.

e) The refrigerant has a specific latent heat of vaporisation of 3×10^6 J/kg, and the specific latent heat of fusion of ice is approximately 3×10^5 J/kg. What mass of water, at 0 °C, can be converted to ice, per kilogram of refrigerant vaporised?

10 While jogging on a level road, your body generates heat energy at the rate of about 900 W. About half of this energy is transferred to the surroundings by evaporating sweat. The specific latent heat of vaporisation of sweat is about 2×10^6 J/kg.

a) Explain how sweating can cool the body.

b) Calculate how much sweat you would lose during 1 hour of jogging.

c) What accounts for the rest of the heat transfer?

d) Is it more comfortable to jog on a dry day or a humid day? (Assume temperature is constant.)

A

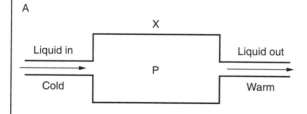

B

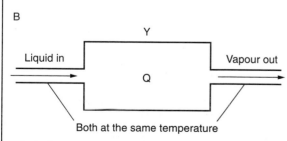

Figure 6

47

Heat transfer

▶ Conduction requires a medium, and takes place without any bulk movement of the medium.
▶ Convection occurs in liquids or gases and involves the bulk movement of particles away from the heat source. For example, if air is heated it expands and becomes less dense than the surrounding, colder air. Gravity causes the cold air to sink and the hot air rises.

▶ Radiation does not require a medium.
▶ Very hot bodies (e.g. the Sun) radiate heat energy in the form of *electromagnetic waves*.
▶ Dull or black surfaces are much better *absorbers* of heat radiation than shiny or white surfaces.
▶ Dull or black surfaces are much better *emitters* of heat radiation than shiny or white surfaces.

Questions

11 *Statement A:* Heat energy is transferred by the large scale movement of the material medium away from the source of heat.

Statement B: Energy, in the form of electromagnetic waves, is emitted from one body and absorbed by another, without the need of any material medium in between.

Statement C: Heat energy, in the form of atomic vibration, is transferred through a material, from regions of high temperature to regions of low temperature, without any large scale movement of the material itself.

a) Which of the three statements describes (i) conduction, (ii) convection, (iii) radiation?

b) Which methods of heat transfer can take place:
i) only in liquids and gases (fluids)?
ii) across empty space?
iii) in solids, liquids and gases, but not across empty space?

12 Explain the following facts:

a) A concrete floor feels much colder than a wooden floor when walked on with bare feet, although the temperature of each floor is the same.

b) Clean snow does not melt very quickly in sunshine, dirty snow does.

c) A string vest containing many holes acts as a very good insulator.

d) After the London marathon athletes are wrapped in aluminium coated plastic sheets.

e) Birds fluff up their feathers in cold weather.

f) Glider pilots can manoeuvre their gliders to great heights, without using an engine.

g) Radiation from the Sun has been falling on the Earth for millions of years, yet the average temperature of the Earth remains steady.

h) A small animal has to eat a far higher proportion of its body weight in food than a larger animal, to maintain the same body temperature (assume similar shape and same surface texture).

i) Convection cannot take place without the help of gravity.

13 Figure 7 shows an experiment for comparing the conductivities of different metals.

a) What must be done to ensure that the experiment is a 'fair test'?

b) List the five conductors in order of conductivity, putting the best conductor first.

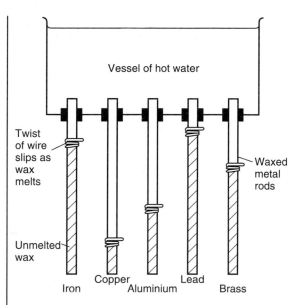

Figure 7

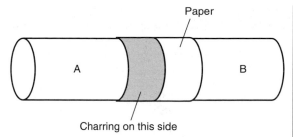

Figure 8

i) Which half is wood and which is brass, A or B?
ii) Explain this effect.

b) Explain the two effects shown in Figures 9 and 10.

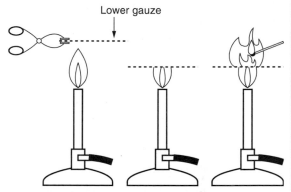

Figure 9 Lowering the gauze on the Bunsen squashes the flame, though above the gauze there is still unburnt gas which can be ignited with a match.

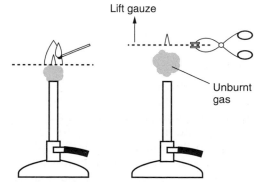

Figure 10 The gas above the gauze can be lit, without lighting the gas below. Lifting the gauze 'lifts' off the flame!

c) Which metal would you choose for making a coal-fire poker: copper or brass? Why?

14 Metals are good conductors of heat and electricity, non-metals are not. If the metals are arranged in order of their *electrical* conductivity, the order is the same as for their *thermal* conductivity.

a) One end of a metal rod is heated.
  i) In what way are the atoms at the hot end different from the atoms at the cold end?
  ii) In what way are the 'free' electrons at the hot end different from those at the cold end?
  iii) What happens to the atoms and 'free' electrons along the bar, over time?

b) Describe how heat energy is transferred along a rod made from a non-metal.

c) Explain why metals are better conductors of heat than non-metals.

15 a) Figure 8 shows a thick rod, half of which is made of wood and half of brass tubing. A strip of white paper is held tightly round the join and the rod is rotated slowly in a Bunsen flame, until the paper starts to char. The paper chars on one side of the join only.

c) Explain using a diagram how a lighted candle can be made safe in an atmosphere containing methane gas.

16 a) Describe simple experiments you could carry out to show that:
i) black surfaces are better absorbers of heat radiation than shiny surfaces.
ii) black surfaces are better emitters of heat radiation than shiny surfaces.
b) How will you make each test 'fair'?

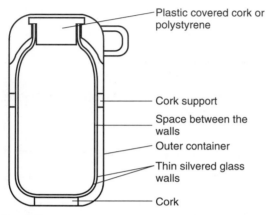

Figure 11 labels: Plastic covered cork or polystyrene; Cork support; Space between the walls; Outer container; Thin silvered glass walls; Cork

Figure 11

17 Figure 11 shows a thermos flask.

a) Explain why the vessel is made with double glass walls.

b) The inner surfaces of the glass walls are silvered. Why?

c) The flask is sometimes called a **vacuum** flask. Where is the vacuum? What purpose does it serve?

d) Despite the vacuum, conduction to the outside can still occur. Explain how making the glass walls thin can reduce heat loss by conduction.

18 Tom and Carol are planting tomato plants inside a greenhouse. There is no wind, and the temperature inside the greenhouse is much greater than outside. Figure 12 shows an absorption graph drawn by Tom. Tom uses the graph to explain why it is so hot inside the greenhouse. It shows that certain wavelengths of radiation from the Sun are absorbed more than others by the glass.

a) How can Tom use the graph to explain why the greenhouse heats up?

b) Why else does the greenhouse heat up?

c) Carol tells Tom that the pollution of the atmosphere is causing the temperature at the Earth's surface to increase.
i) Explain why this effect is called the 'greenhouse' effect.
ii) Which are the principle gases responsible for this effect?

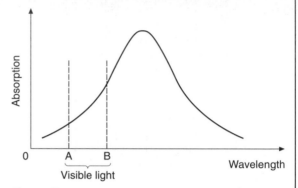

Figure 12 axes: Absorption (vertical); Wavelength (horizontal); A B Visible light

Figure 12

19 Sarah and Kate rent an apartment in Greece with a large solar heating panel on the roof. Sarah explains to Kate how it works using Figure 13.

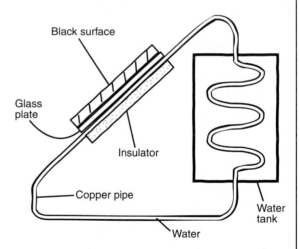

Figure 13 labels: Black surface; Glass plate; Insulator; Copper pipe; Water; Water tank

Figure 13 Solar panel.

a) i) Why does the solar panel have a black surface?
ii) Why is the pipework in the water tank twisted?

b) i) Describe the process by which the water in the pipe heats up.
ii) Why does it circulate?

c) Describe the process by which the water in the storage tank heats up.

7 Waves and Sound

Waves

▶ In transverse waves particles oscillate at *right angles* to the direction of travel.
▶ In longitudinal waves particles oscillate *parallel* to the direction of travel.
▶ The frequency of an oscillating object is the number of oscillations it completes each second.
▶ The frequency of a wave is the number of complete waves produced each second.
▶ The time period of an oscillating object is the time for one oscillation.
▶ The time period of a wave is the time to produce one complete wave.

▶ Wave speed is the distance travelled by a wave in 1 second. Wave speed can be calculated from:
wave speed = frequency × wavelength
▶ Amplitude and wavelength:

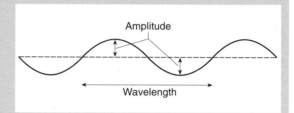

Questions ❔❔❔❔❔❔❔❔❔❔❔❔❔❔❔

1 Alex and Ivan are playing with a slinky stretched over a wooden floor. Alex sends a transverse wave along the slinky, which takes 3 seconds to reach Ivan (Figure 1).

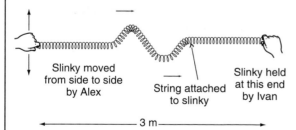

Figure 1

a) How does Alex have to move his hand to produce this wave?

b) Describe the motion of the piece of string as the wave passes.

c) Explain the meaning of the word *transverse*.

d) Calculate the speed of the wave.

e) Ivan moves to 4 m away from Alex. They find that another similar wave reaches Ivan in 3.5 seconds.
i) What effect does the move have on wave speed?
ii) What effect does tension have on wave speed?

f) Alex says he is transferring energy to Ivan. In what form is this energy?

g) How can Ivan tell that energy is being transferred, while keeping his eyes shut?

h) Draw a picture of the slinky to show what it would look like when the wave has been reflected back from Ivan's hand.

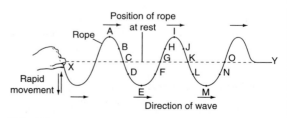

Figure 2

51

2 a) All the labelled points in Figure 2 (see page 51) are seen to oscillate as the waves pass. What does *oscillate* mean?

b) In what direction are the following points moving:
(i) B, (ii) D, (iii) F, (iv) H?

c) Which points are stationary at the instant shown?

d) In which direction are the following points about to move:
(i) A, (ii) E, (iii) I, (iv) M?

e) Points A and I oscillate *in phase* with each other. What does *in phase* mean?

f) Which of the labelled points are oscillating in phase with:
(i) E, (ii) G, (iii) B, (iv) the hand at X?

3 In Figure 3A, end X of a long rope has been waggled up and down four times to produce four waves in 2 seconds. The waves occupy 8 m of rope and travel towards Y at constant speed.

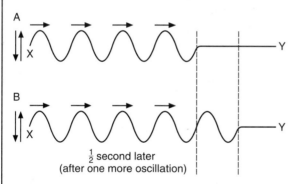

Figure 3

a) Calculate the *time-period* of the wave motion (time for one complete oscillation).

b) Calculate the *frequency* of the wave motion (number of oscillations per second).

c) What is the relationship between the time-period and the frequency?

d) Calculate the *wavelength* of the wave motion (length of one complete wave).

e) During the next $\frac{1}{2}$ second, end X is waggled once more to make one more wave (Figure 3B). How far does the leading wave move in this time?

f) Calculate the speed of the leading wave.

4 End A of the rope in Figure 4 is being waggled up and down at a rate of five oscillations every 2 seconds.

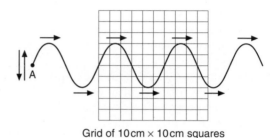

Grid of 10 cm × 10 cm squares

Figure 4

a) Find the *amplitude* of the wave motion (maximum displacement to one side).

b) Find the *wavelength*.

c) Calculate the *time-period*.

d) Calculate the *frequency*.

e) How far do the waves travel during one time-period?

f) Calculate the wave speed.

5 Alex moves his hand rapidly to produce *longitudinal* waves along the slinky (Figure 5).

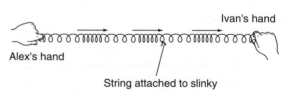

Alex's hand

Ivan's hand

String attached to slinky

Figure 5

a) How did Alex move his hand to produce these waves?

b) Describe the motion of the piece of string as each wave passes.

c) Explain the meaning of the word *longitudinal*.

d) Why are these waves sometimes called *compression* waves?

e) How can Ivan tell that energy is being transferred, while keeping his eyes shut?

f) Copy the slinky in Figure 5 and indicate two points which are one wavelength apart.

7 Explain the following.

a) Longitudinal waves can travel *through* gases, solids and liquids, but transverse waves can only travel *through* solids.

b) A transverse wave can travel *along the surface* of a liquid.

c) An earthquake at point X in Figure 7 acts as a source of longitudinal and transverse waves. Both types of wave are detected at seismic stations A, B and C, but only longitudinal waves are detected at D.

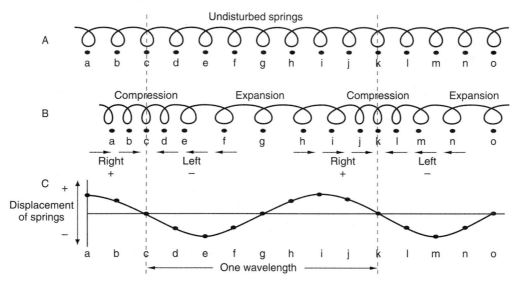

Figure 6

6 If you draw a graph for longitudinal waves with displacements to the left and right along the *y*-axis, and distance along the *x*-axis, you can see their *waviness*. Figure 6A–C shows this.

a) Which points in Figure 6C indicate
   i) maximum displacement to the right?
   ii) maximum displacement to the left?
   iii) the centre of a compression?
   iv) the centre of an expansion?

b) Sketch the graph and then sketch another graph to represent the state of the slinky after the wave has moved quarter of a wavelength to the right.

c) Looking at the two graphs, work out the direction points c and g must be moving in Figure 6B.

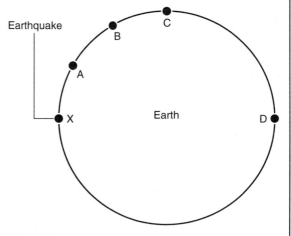

Figure 7

8 Sita tells Samantha that sound passing through air is an example of a longitudinal wave.

53

a) Describe an experiment to show that:
i) sources of sound vibrate
ii) sound needs a medium (e.g. air) to carry it.

b) Describe how sound energy is produced by a drummer striking a drum, transmitted through the air and heard by a listener.

9 a) The length of a railway carriage is 28 m. An observer at the station counts ten carriages passing him in 14 seconds. How fast is the train travelling?

b) Deep sea waves pass under an anchored yacht at a rate of five crests every 20 seconds. The distance from crest to crest is 8 m. What speed are the waves travelling?

c) If a source of waves emits f waves every second, and the distance between each wave is λ, how would you calculate the distance travelled by the waves in one second?

d) Refer to part (b).
i) At what frequency does the yacht bob up and down?
ii) What is the wavelength of the waves?
iii) Using the formula $v = f\lambda$, calculate the speed of the water waves.

10 Wendy and Shaun have fixed a strobe (flashing light) above a ripple tank so that the light illuminates the water surface (Figure 8). The ripples appear to be stationary when the strobe frequency is 30 Hz, but not at higher frequencies.

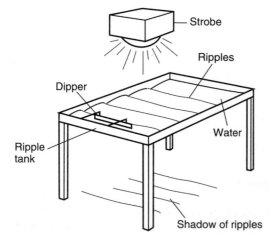

a) Why do the ripples appear to be stationary?

b) If the frequency of the strobe is increased a little, the ripples appear to move slowly backwards. Why?

c) What strobe adjustment would make the ripples appear to move forward?

d) What is the frequency of the dipper?

e) By looking at the stationary pattern, Shaun estimates that the ripples are 2 cm apart. Calculate the speed of the ripples.

f) In shallower water, ripples from the same source appear closer together. What does this tell you about their speed?

11 Copy and complete the diagrams in Figure 9. In each case, add three more waves: one being reflected and two after reflection. Indicate with dotted arrows their direction of travel.

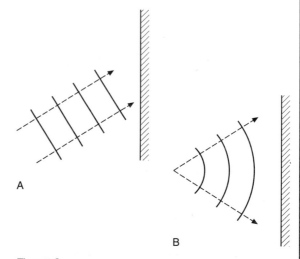

Figure 9

12 When water waves cross over from a region of deeper water to shallower water, their speed decreases. Their wavelength changes too and, if they approach the boundary at an angle, their direction changes. Copy and complete the diagrams in Figure 10 to show these two effects. In each case, add three more waves: one crossing the boundary and two which have crossed the boundary. Show their direction of travel.

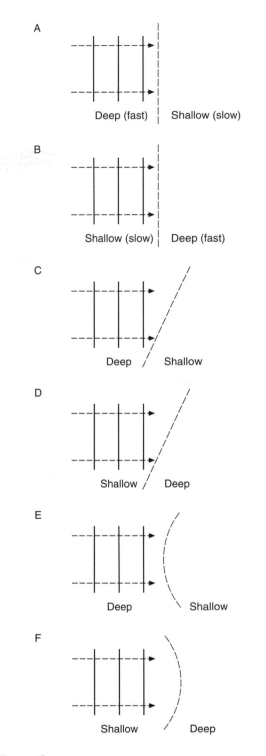

A

Deep (fast) | Shallow (slow)

B

Shallow (slow) | Deep (fast)

C

Deep / Shallow

D

Shallow / Deep

E

Deep \ Shallow

F

Shallow / Deep

Figure 10

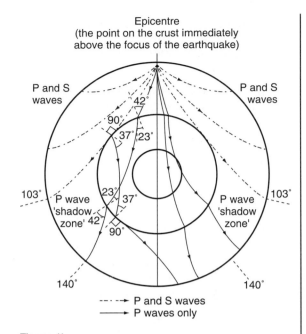

Epicentre
(the point on the crust immediately
above the focus of the earthquake)

P and S waves

P and S waves

42°

90°

37° 23°

103°

P wave 'shadow zone'

23° 37°

42°

90°

P wave 'shadow zone'

103°

140°

140°

- - - → P and S waves
——→ P waves only

Figure 11

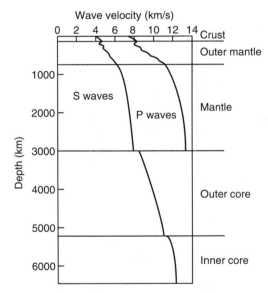

Wave velocity (km/s)

0 2 4 6 8 10 12 14 Crust

Outer mantle

1000

S waves

P waves

2000

Mantle

3000

Depth (km)

4000

Outer core

5000

6000

Inner core

Figure 12

13 Figure 11 shows paths of seismic P (longitudinal) and S (transverse) waves through the Earth, Figure 12 shows how the speed of the waves changes with depth.

a) A seismic station detects P and S waves from an earthquake. Explain which type of wave is detected first.

b) In Figure 11 you can see that P waves which enter the core always change direction. Use the information in Figure 12 to explain why.

55

c) S waves do not travel in the outer core. What can you deduce about the nature of the outer core from this?

14 Figure 13 shows what happens when straight waves in a ripple tank pass through an aperture and diffract. The angle of spread (A) depends on the size of the aperture (S) and the wavelength (λ). The smaller the aperture the greater the angle; the shorter the wavelength the greater the angle.

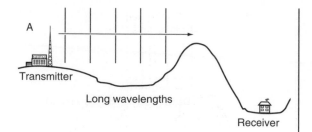

Long wavelengths

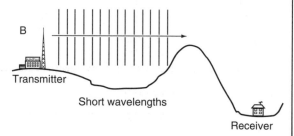

Short wavelengths

Figure 14

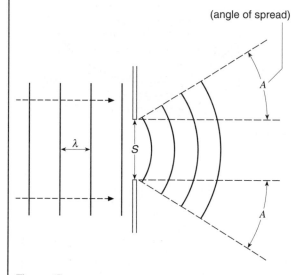

Figure 13

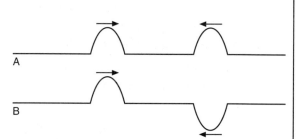

Figure 15

a) Draw a diagram like Figure 13 to show the effect of (i) decreasing the aperture (ii) reducing wavelength.

b) Draw a diagram like Figure 13 to show how waves with different wavelengths bend round barriers.

15 a) Sound diffracts. If you listen to an orchestra through an open doorway to a concert hall you tend to hear only the bass instruments, not the treble. Why?

b) Light waves do not appear to diffract through apertures or bend around obstacles. Why might this be? What do you need to do to get light to diffract?

c) Radio waves diffract. Figure 14 shows a radio station which can transmit waves of both long and short wavelengths. Which of the two wavelengths can be detected by a receiver in the valley? Explain why. Use diagrams to help you.

16 a) Figure 15A shows two identical humps travelling in opposite directions along a rope. Draw diagrams to show what the rope will look like (i) when the humps meet (ii) some time after they have met.

b) Figure 15B shows a hump and trough travelling in opposite directions. Draw diagrams to show what the rope will look like (i) when the humps meet (ii) some time after they have met.

17 Figure 16 shows two dippers acting as coherent sources of waves in a ripple tank. The waves cross each other and interfere. The resultant motion of the bead depends on the path difference (BP–AP).

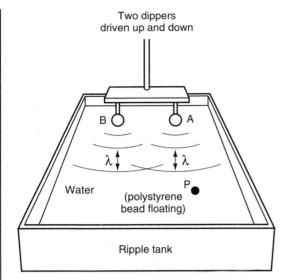

Two dippers driven up and down

B   A

λ λ

Water   P

(polystyrene bead floating)

Ripple tank

Figure 16

a) What does the word *coherent* mean?

b) What does the word *interfere* mean? Explain how this interference can be *constructive* or *destructive*.

c) What is meant by *path difference*?

d) Why does the motion of the bead depend on path difference?

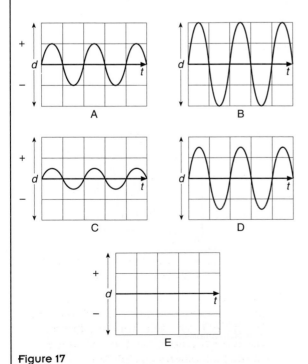

Figure 17

e) Figure 17A is a displacement–time graph for the motion of the bead when only one of the dippers is in use. The bead can be placed at different points on the surface to vary the path difference. Which of the displacement–time graphs in Figure 17, best illustrates the motion of the bead when the path difference (BP–AP) is:
   i)   zero?
   ii) half a wavelength?
   iii) one wavelength?
   iv) one and a half wavelengths?
   v)   two wavelengths?
   vi) quarter of a wavelength?
   vii) three quarters of a wavelength?

18 Figure 18 shows two dippers, X and Y, which oscillate up and down in a ripple tank to form ripples. The speed of the ripples is 2.4 m/s.

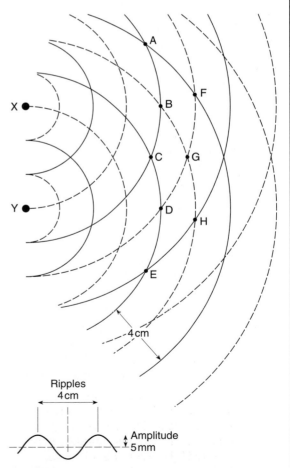

4 cm

Ripples
4 cm

Amplitude
5 mm

Figure 18

57

a) When both dippers oscillate in phase, which labelled points show:
   (i) constructive interference
   (ii) destructive interference?

b) What will be the amplitude of ripples at points marked B, C and G?

c) What will be the amplitude at these points if the dippers oscillate in antiphase?

d) If the distance of point A from dipper X is 8 cm, how far must A be from dipper Y?

e) Calculate the frequency of the dippers.

f) Suppose the frequency of the dippers is doubled:
   i) What effect will this have on the wavelength and the speed of the ripples?
   ii) What effect will this have on the spacing of points A, B, C, D and E?

Sound

▶ Sound waves are longitudinal and require a medium to carry them.

▶ The energy of a sound wave depends on its amplitude.

▶ Loudness depends on the amplitude of the wave, and on the sensitivity of the listener's ear.

▶ The pitch of a musical note depends on frequency. The higher the frequency, the higher the pitch.

▶ The quality of a musical note depends on the shape of the waveform.

▶ The **Doppler effect**: the waves in front of a moving source become bunched and the waves behind it become stretched out. In the case of sound waves, this results in a change of pitch as the source passes by.

Questions

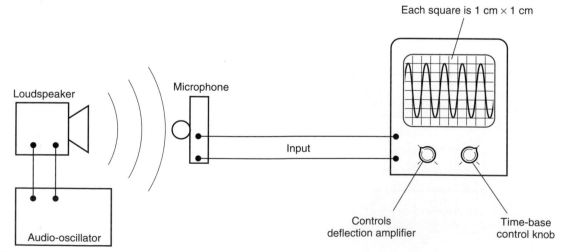

Figure 19

58

19 The time-base of the CRO in Figure 19 is set at 2 ms/cm (i.e. each centimetre of trace across the screen takes 2 milliseconds).

a) How many complete oscillations are on the screen?

b) Each oscillation is caused by a sound wave reaching the microphone. How many sound waves are emitted by the loudspeaker each second?

c) What is the frequency of the sound source?

d) The speed of sound in air is 340 m/s. Calculate the wavelength of the sound waves.

e) Are sound waves longitudinal or transverse?

f) A friend says that rotating the speaker onto its side will reduce the amplitude of the trace. Is this correct? Why?

g) The loudspeaker is moved towards the microphone and the amplitude of the trace is seen to fluctuate between maxima and minima. Why?

20 The depth of a liquid in an industrial container can be checked using ultrasound (Figure 20A). Some of the ultrasound emitted by the transducer is reflected back from the surface.

a) What is the difference between ultrasound and ordinary sound?

b) Why is it better to use ultrasound for this measurement?

c) What is meant by a *pulse*?

d) Explain why the first pulse (Figure 20B), is bigger than the second.

e) Work out the time between the emitted pulse and the received pulse.

f) If the speed of ultrasound through the liquid is 1500 m/s, calculate the depth of the liquid.

g) If the frequency of the ultrasound is 50 kHz, what is its wavelength?

21 A source of sound has a frequency of 330 Hz. Its wavelength is 1 m.

a) How far apart is each compression?

b) How many compressions are produced in 1 second?

c) How far will the first compression travel in 1 second?

d) According to these calculations, what is the velocity of sound through air?

22 Figure 21 illustrates the **Doppler effect**. When a source of sound waves moves, the waves in front become bunched, and the waves behind stretch out.

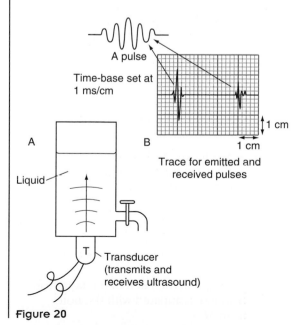

Figure 20

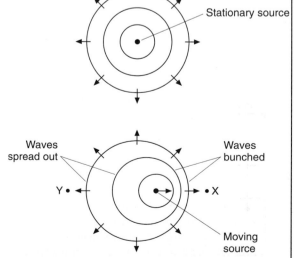

Figure 21

59

a) Explain why the waves in front become bunched.

b) Explain why the waves behind become stretched out.

c) Suppose the frequency of the sound waves is 500 Hz.
i) Will the frequency of the sound heard by an observer at point X be higher than, lower than, or equal to 500 Hz?
ii) What about at point Y?

d) An ambulance rushes past you in the street, sounding its siren. Imagine that you are standing half way along the street. Describe how the note of the siren would appear to change, as the ambulance moves along the street.

e) The Doppler effect accounts for the 'red shift' seen in the light coming from distance stars which are moving away from us.
i) Explain in terms of the Doppler effect what this *red shift* is.
ii) What do you think causes a *blue shift*?

23 A Formula One racing car is travelling at 80 m/s. Its engine emits a high pitched sound at 200 Hz. The speed of sound in air is 330 m/s. Thinking about the waves emitted in the forward direction:

a) How many sound waves are emitted in 1 second?

b) How far does the first wave travel in 1 second?

c) How far does the car travel in 1 second?

d) Calculate the distance separating the first wave and the car, after 1 second.

e) Calculate the distance between each wave in front of the car.

f) Use the formula $v = f\lambda$ to work out the apparent frequency of the waves heard by an observer some distance in front of the car.

24 The human ear can detect continuous sounds in the frequency range 20 Hz to 20 000 Hz. Figure 22 shows how air pressure next to the ear drum varies with time, for a 20 Hz note.

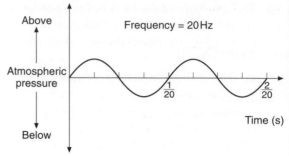

Figure 22

a) Sound waves travel at 330 m/s. Calculate the range of wavelengths which correspond to these frequencies.

b) A series of sharp pulses with a frequency below 20 Hz can be heard, but not as a continuous note. Draw graphs similar to Figure 22 to show how a continuous note at 20 Hz is different from sharp pulses at 20 Hz.

25 In Figure 23, the toothed wheel A rotates 10 times per second, causing the clamped card to vibrate. This produces a high pitched note.

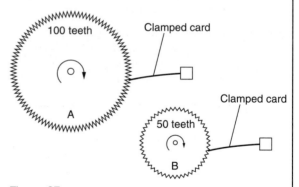

Figure 23

a) Calculate the frequency of the note from the vibrating card.

b) As the toothed wheel slows down:
i) how will the frequency of the vibrating card change?
ii) how will the pitch change?

c) Wheel B has only 50 teeth. If it rotates at the same rate as A:
i) calculate the frequency of the note produced
ii) how will the pitch of the note from B sound, compared with the note from A?

d) If wheel A is rotated at half the rate of B, how will the notes compare? Why?

e) If alternate teeth are missing from wheel A, and both wheels rotate at the same rate, how will the notes compare?

26 Tracy connects a microphone to an oscilloscope to look at the waveforms obtained from a demonstration CD. She observes four different traces (Figure 24).

a) Which note, A or B, has the higher pitch? Why?

b) Which note is louder, B or C? Why?

c) Why can't you tell whether A is louder than C, but you can tell that D is louder than A?

d) Which notes could have been made with the same instrument? Why?

e) How do notes C and D compare, with regard to pitch and quality?

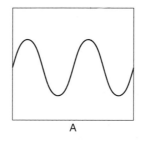
A

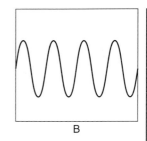
B

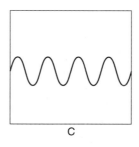
C

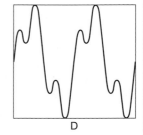
D

Figure 24

Electromagnetic waves

▶ Electromagnetic waves travel through a vacuum at the speed of light (3×10^8 m/s).

▶ Electromagnetic waves consist of rapidly changing magnetic and electric fields.

▶ Visible light, heat radiation, radio waves, ultra-violet radiation, and X-rays are all examples of electromagnetic waves.

Questions ❓❓❓❓❓❓❓❓❓❓❓❓❓❓❓

27 Figure 25 shows the spectrum of electromagnetic waves (not drawn to scale!). Which regions correspond most closely to:
(i) visible light? (ii) ultra-violet? (iii) TV waves? (iv) radio waves? (v) microwaves? (vi) infra-red? (vii) X-rays?

28 In Figure 26 (see page 62) a laser beam is directed onto a screen (A), through a small slit about 0.05 mm wide (B), and through two small slits about 0.2 mm apart (C).

a) Explain why these experiments support the theory that light is a wave motion.

b) Why does the slit have to be so small in B?

10^{-11} m	10^{-9} m	4×10^{-7} m	7×10^{-7} m	10^{-3} m	10^{-1} m	10 m	10^4 m
a	b	c	d	e	f	g	

Figure 25

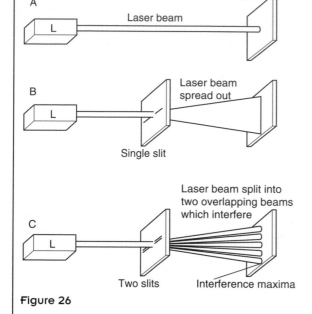

Figure 26

c) What is this effect called?

d) Why do the slits have to be so close together in C?

e) How is the distance between the maxima affected if, in diagram C,
i) the slits are closer together?
ii) the screen is positioned further away?
iii) the laser emits light of longer wavelength?

29 Non-reflective spectacle lenses are coated with a very thin transparent film so that some of the light striking the lens is reflected from the air–film interface, and some from the film–glass interface. By choosing the right thickness of film, the reflected light can be made to interfere destructively. This idea is shown in Figure 27.

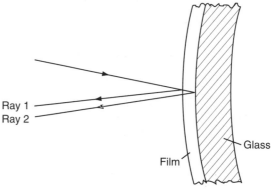

Figure 27

a) What does destructive interference mean?

b) Why should the two *rays* of reflected light interfere destructively?

c) There is a path difference between the two reflected rays. In terms of λ how much further must ray 2 have travelled, if it is to cancel out ray 1?

Communication

▶ Waves can be used to carry information as well as energy.

▶ Information can be sent using a carrier wave by:
i) varying the amplitude – amplitude modulation (AM);
ii) varying the frequency – frequency modulation (FM).

▶ A carrier wave is the transmitted wave, with no information on it; its frequency and amplitude are constant.

▶ Analogue signals can be represented by voltages which vary continuously with time and produce the same waveform as the source.

▶ Digital signals can be represented by voltages which do not vary continuously, but have two specific levels, high or low. The information is encoded in the form of a series of pulses.

▶ Electrical noise is the distortion of a signal by unwanted electrical disturbances. The advantage of digital signalling is that weak pulses can be regenerated without noise. In analogue signalling, a weak waveform can be amplified, but the noise is amplified too.

▶ Communication satellites are put in geostationary orbits so that they remain over the same point on the rotating Earth's surface. The satellites orbit the Equator at a height of about 36 000 km, and take 24 hours to orbit the Earth.

▶ Earth observation satellites are put into polar orbits, passing over the poles at heights ranging from 100 km to 6400 km. These satellites do not stay over the same point on the Earth's surface. They orbit Earth several times each day.

Questions

30 All waves transfer energy and can carry information. What type of wave is used to transmit and receive messages by:
  i) signalling to a friend with a torch?
  ii) shouting at a friend?
  iii) using a mobile phone?

32 a) Figure 29A shows an AM carrier wave. Using the same scale, sketch the shape of:
  i) the wave before it was modulated
  ii) the signal received after detection.

A

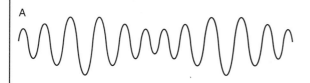

B

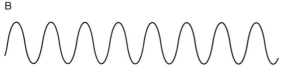

C

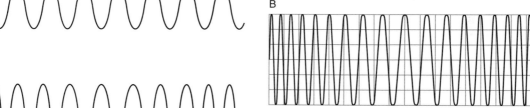

Figure 28

A

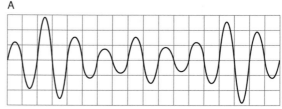

B

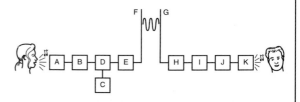

Figure 29

31 Look at the three waveforms in Figure 28.

a) Which waveform represents a carrier wave with no information on it?

b) Describe how information is carried by the other two waveforms?

c) In radio, what do AM and FM stand for?

d) Which carrier wave has the higher frequency, AM or FM?

e) Why can AM waves bend round the Earth's surface, but FM cannot?

f) Why is FM sometimes referred to as a 'line of sight' radio wave?

b) Figure 29B shows an FM carrier wave. Using the same scale, sketch the shape of:
  i) the wave before it was modulated
  ii) the signal received after detection.

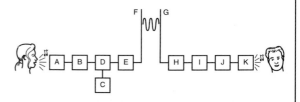

Figure 30

63

33 a) Figure 30 (see page 63) shows how AM radio waves are transmitted and received. Match each block with one of the following:

an input transducer
two AF amplifiers
a carrier signal source
an encoder
two RF amplifiers
a transmitting aerial
a receiving aerial
a decoder
an output transducer

b) Which items listed in part (a) could be:
   i) a microphone?
   ii) a loudspeaker?
   iii) a diode detector circuit?
   iv) a modulator circuit?

34 Information can be encoded into digital form. One example of this is pulse code modulation (PCM). The amplitude of a message signal is sampled at regular intervals. Each value of the amplitude is transmitted as a series of pulses which represent a binary number.

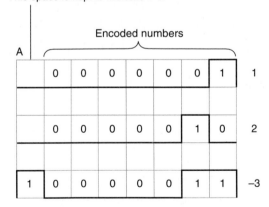

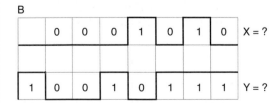

Figure 31

a) The series of pulses in Figure 31A are eight-bit binary codes for 1, 2 and −3. Decode the pulses in Figure 31B.

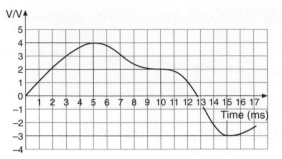

Figure 32

b) Figure 32 shows a signal wave form sampled every millisecond.
   i) Write down the voltage levels at 5 ms, 10 ms and 15 ms.
   ii) Encode these voltages by expressing them as binary numbers.
   iii) Draw eight-bit pulse diagrams to show how this information would be transmitted.

35 In Figure 33 electrical signals at X travel to Y along a long cable. Between X and Y the signals are attenuated and pick up 'noise'. The signals then pass through either a repeater or a regenerator, depending on whether they are in digital or analogue form.

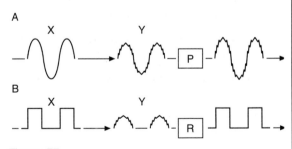

Figure 33

a) What does *attenuation* mean? Why does it occur?

b) What is meant by the term *noise*? What causes it?

c) Explain the difference between an analogue and a digital signal.

d) Which box is a *repeater*? Which is a *regenerator*? How can you tell?

e) What is the advantage of sending digital signals instead of analogue?

36 There are several routes that radio waves can take between transmitters and receivers around the Earth. Waves are given the names sky waves, space waves and ground waves.

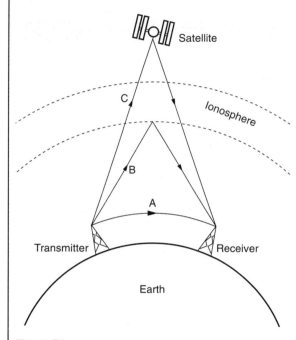

Figure 34

a) What are the names of the waves taking routes A, B and C in Figure 34?

b) Which waves have frequencies less than 2 MHz?

c) Which waves have frequencies in the range of 3–30 MHz?

d) Which waves have frequencies above 30 MHz?

e) What is the ionosphere?

f) Which waves are affected by changes in the ionosphere?

37 Communication satellites can be *passive* or *active*, and they can have *polar*, *equatorial* or *geostationary orbits*.

a) Explain the difference between *passive* and *active* satellites.

b) What is a *geostationary orbit*? Name an example of a geostationary satellite.

c) What are polar orbiting satellites used for?

d) An Earth observation satellite, in polar orbit, passes overhead every 90 minutes. How many times does it pass over in one day?

e) Signals transmitted to Earth from orbiting satellites spread out because of diffraction. How can this effect be minimised?

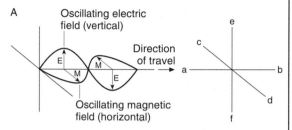

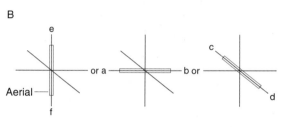

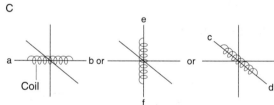

Figure 35

38 Figure 35A shows an electromagnetic wave travelling from left to right. The wave is plane polarised. Energy from the wave can be picked up by an aerial rod, or a coil. The coil is wound on a ferrite rod.

a) What does *plane polarised* mean?

b) Along which direction should the aerial rod be aligned in Figure 35B?

c) Along which direction should the coil be aligned in Figure 35C?

d) What is an alternating current?

e) Explain how small alternating electric currents are produced:
   i) in the aerial rod
   ii) in the coil.

f) What is the purpose of the ferrite rod?

65

8 Light and Optics

Shadows

▶ A point source of light forms a sharp shadow of an object.

▶ An eclipse of the Sun occurs when the Moon comes between the Earth and the Sun.

▶ An eclipse of the Moon occurs when the Earth comes between the Moon and the Sun.

▶ The Moon is a non-luminous body and can only be seen because it reflects light from the Sun.

▶ The apparent changes in shape of the Moon, during the course of each month, arise because we see only the illuminated region. The amount we can see varies with the Moon's position.

Questions

1 Tom and Jo are trying to see if light travels in straight lines. To do this they put a lamp in a box, with a small hole and shine the light towards a card to form a shadow (Figure 1).

a) How big will the shadow be if light travels in straight lines?

b) Why did they put the lamp in a box with a small hole?

c) Draw a ray diagram to show how the shadow would change if the box was removed.

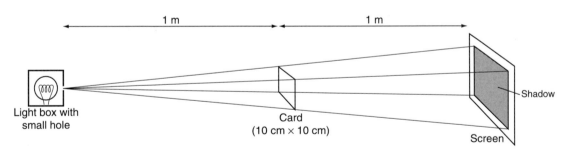

Figure 1

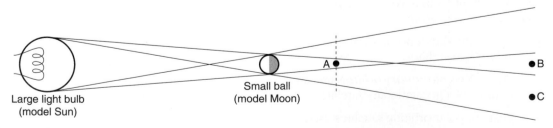

66 | Figure 2

2 A demonstration is set up in the laboratory to show different kinds of eclipses of the Sun. The Sun is represented by a large bowl type lamp (Figure 2) and the Moon by a polystyrene ball. Students are asked to look at the model Sun from different points (A, B, C) behind the model Moon.

a) Will they be able to see any part of the Sun from position A? Draw a diagram to show what they will see.

b) Draw a diagram to show what the Sun will look like from position B.

c) From which of the positions is the eclipse:
(i) ring-like? (ii) total? (iii) partial?

d) Draw a diagram to show where a model Earth should be placed to demonstrate the shadow formed on its surface by a total eclipse of the Sun.

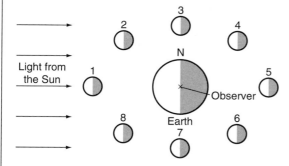

Figure 3

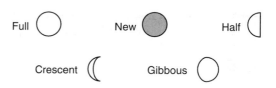

Figure 4

3 Figure 3 shows why the appearance of the Moon changes during a lunar month. Gary lives in the northern hemisphere. He makes some sketches of the Moon at night as its shape changes (Figure 4).

a) Which of Gary's sketches were made when the Moon was in:
(i) position 1? (ii) position 2?
(iii) position 3? (iv) position 5?

b) Sketch what Gary might have seen when the Moon was in:
(i) position 6 (ii) position 7.

c) What property of light causes the Moon to be visible?

d) Sometimes when the Moon passes through position 5, it cannot be seen at night, even if the sky is cloudless. Why?

4 Sam and Eric make a model pin-hole camera (Figure 5). They use it to look at a building.

a) What is the greaseproof paper for?

b) Why is it necessary to look at the screen through a peep-hole?

c) Draw a diagram to show how light from points A, B and C reach the translucent screen.

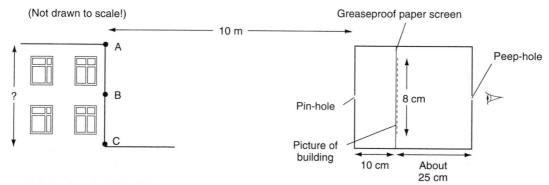

Figure 5

d) Explain why a picture of the building is formed. Describe its appearance (will it be upside down or the right way up, enlarged or diminished?).

e) Sam thinks he can get a better picture by enlarging the pin-hole. Is he right? Explain your answer, using ray diagrams.

f) Eric decides to move the camera closer to the building. What effect will this have on the picture?

g) Using Figure 5 (page 67), calculate the building's height.

h) How would you turn the model camera into a real pin-hole camera?

Reflection and images

▶ The incident ray, the reflected ray and the normal all lie in the same plane.
▶ The angle of incidence = the angle of reflection.
▶ The rays of light from points on an object appear to be coming from corresponding points behind a mirror after reflection. What you see is called an image.

▶ The image seen in a plane mirror is always directly opposite the object, and the same distance behind the mirror as the object is in front of the mirror.

Questions

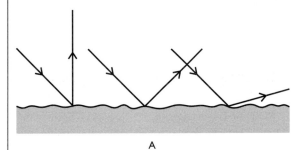

A

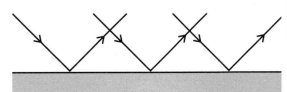

B

Figure 6

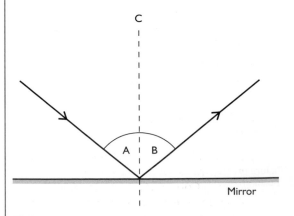

Figure 7

5 a) Which of the diagrams in Figure 6 shows:
(i) regular reflection (ii) irregular reflection?

b) Figure 7 shows how a narrow beam of light is reflected from a plane mirror.
i) What is the dashed line C called?
ii) What are the angles A and B called?
iii) What can you always say about angles A and B?

c) If you look at light from the Moon reflecting in a lake you see a beam. If you look at the light in a plane mirror, you see a clear image of the Moon. Why?

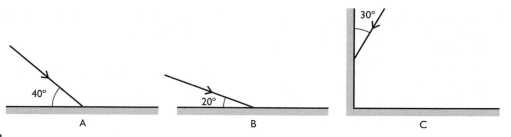

Figure 8

6 a) Copy and complete Figure 8 to show how light is reflected from the plane mirrors. In each case mark the angles between the reflected ray and the mirror.

b) It is better to measure the angle between these rays and the *normal* to the mirror. Suggest why this might be preferable.

c) Copy diagrams A and B again, only this time draw in the normal and the reflected rays, and mark the values of the angles between each ray and the normal.

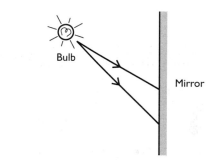

Figure 10

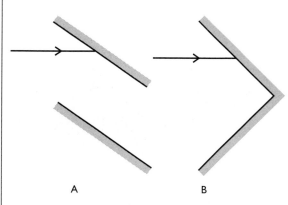

Figure 9

7 a) Figure 9 shows two mirrors arranged either at right angles, or in parallel. Copy each diagram and draw in the path each ray takes after reflection.

b) Which diagram shows the action of a periscope?

c) If you wanted light *always* to be reflected straight back to its source which arrangement would you use? Name a situation where this could be useful.

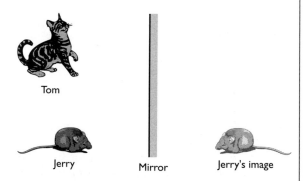

Figure 11

8 Study Figure 10.

a) Copy and complete the diagram, to show the paths of the reflected rays. (Use a protractor to make the drawing accurate.)

b) Trace back the reflected rays with a dotted line, to show where they meet behind the mirror.

c) Why is the point in (b) called a *virtual image*?

d) Figure 11 shows Tom (the cat) looking at the image of Jerry (the mouse) in a mirror. Copy and add rays to the diagram to explain why Tom sees Jerry's image behind the mirror.

Refraction

▶ When a light ray travelling through air hits a glass block at an angle, the ray changes direction. The light ray bends *towards* the normal when it enters the glass, and *away from* the normal when it leaves the glass.

▶ If waves slow down, or speed up, their direction of travel changes, e.g. when they cross the barrier between two different media.

Questions ❓ ❓ ❓ ❓ ❓ ❓ ❓ ❓ ❓ ❓ ❓ ❓ ❓

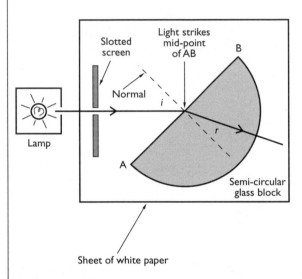

Figure 12

d) What would you expect to happen if the light ray hit the glass travelling along the normal (i.e. angle $i = 0$)? Does your graph predict this? Draw a ray diagram to show the light path through the block.

e) Use your graph to show what will happen when angle i is close to $90°$.

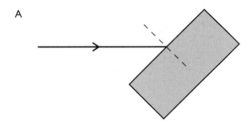

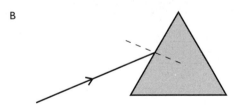

Figure 13

9 Figure 12 shows an experiment for studying light refraction as light crosses from air into glass. Rachel measures the two angles, i, the angle in incidence, and r, the angle of refraction, and records their values for different positions of the glass block (Table 1).

Angle i	25	30	42	50	67	80
Angle r	16	19	26	30	37	40

Table 1

a) The light changes direction on entering the block, but not when leaving. Why?

b) What would happen if the light ray from the lamp did not strike the mid-point? Draw a diagram to show this.

c) Draw a graph of angle r (y-axis) against i (x-axis).

10 a) What is meant by *monochromatic* light?

b) Is white light monochromatic?

c) Copy and complete Figure 13 to show the paths that monochromatic light takes through:
   i) a parallel sided glass block
   ii) a glass prism.

d) When white light passes through a prism, all the colours of the rainbow can be seen. Looking at Figure 14, which light slows down more on entering the glass prism, red or blue? How can you tell?

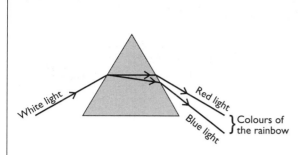

Figure 14

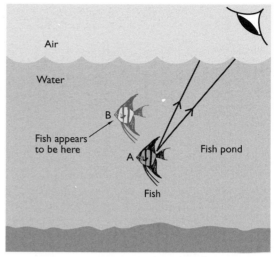

Figure 15

11 Jack stands on the edge of a pond to look at a fish. The fish appears nearer the surface than it is. Peter says that this is because of refraction and explains this with a ray diagram. Part of Peter's diagram is shown in Figure 15.

a) Copy and complete Figure 15 to show how refraction makes the fish appear to be at point B.

b) What causes the light to change direction?

c) Peter shows Jack an experiment he did at school. He places a coin in a shallow bowl and asks Jack to walk away from the bowl until Jack can no longer see the coin. Peter then pours water into the bowl. As the water level rises, Jack sees the coin again. Draw a diagram to explain this effect.

Lenses

- ▶ Converging lenses are thicker in the middle.
- ▶ Diverging lens are thinner in the middle.
- ▶ The principal axis passes through the centre of a lens, normal to the lens surface.
- ▶ For a converging lens, all light rays parallel to the principal axis are converged to a point called the focus of the lens.

- ▶ The focal length is the distance from the centre of the lens to the focus.
- ▶ A real image point is formed when converging rays meet after leaving a lens.
- ▶ A virtual image point is the point from which rays leaving a lens appear to diverge (the lens can be a converging or diverging lens).

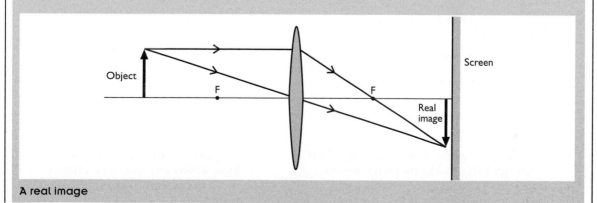

A real image

71

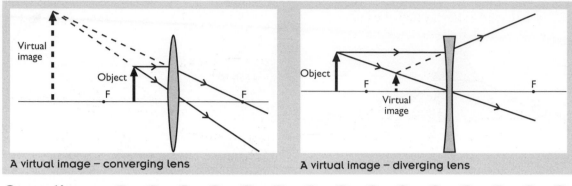

A virtual image – converging lens

A virtual image – diverging lens

Questions ❔ ❔ ❔ ❔ ❔ ❔ ❔ ❔ ❔ ❔ ❔ ❔ ❔ ❔ ❔

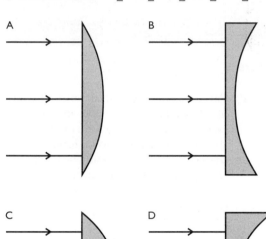

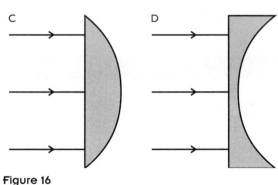

Figure 16

12 a) Copy and complete the ray diagrams in Figure 16 to show how light emerges from the various lenses.

  b) Which lens:
  (i) converges light? (ii) diverges light?

  c) Which is the most strongly converging lens? Why?

  d) Which is the most strongly diverging lens? Why?

  e) If you put equally strong converging and diverging lenses together what would you expect to happen to light passing through them?

13 Figure 17A shows an experiment for testing the properties of a converging lens.

A

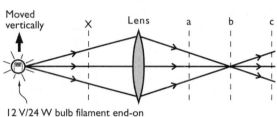

12 V/24 W bulb filament end-on
(to act as a point source of light)

B

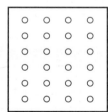

Figure 17

  a) Describe what you would see on a screen placed at a, b and then c.

  b) A board containing holes (see Figure 17B) is inserted at X, between the lamp and the lens. Sketch what would be seen on a screen placed at a, b and then c.

  c) Where do you have to place the screen to obtain an image of the lamp filament?

  d) Describe what happens to the image on the screen when the lamp is moved vertically upwards.

  e) Suppose the lamp is moved towards the lens. Which way would you have to move the screen to keep the image in focus?

14 Figure 18A is the same experiment as in question 13, only this time the bulb filament is vertical.

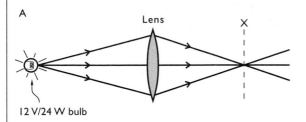

A

12 V/24 W bulb

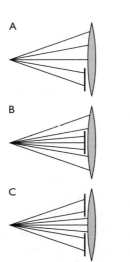

B

Figure 18

a) What is seen on a screen placed at X?

b) We can think of each part of the filament as a point source. Suppose you select three points, P, Q and R (Figure 18B). Redraw Figure 18A to show what happens to two rays from P, two rays from R, and two rays from Q.

c) Now explain what is seen on the screen placed at X. Why is this called an image?

d) Describe and explain what would happen to the image if half the lens is covered, as shown in each of the diagrams in Figure 19.

Figure 19

15 Figure 20 shows a parallel light beam being converged by a lens to a point F, called the *focus*.

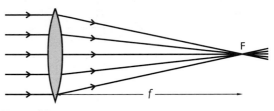

Figure 20

a) What is the distance f called?

b) How does the distance f depend on the shape of the lens?

c) The reciprocal of f (i.e. $1/f$) is an important quantity. Why?

d) Lucy bought a lens which came from a box labelled $+10$ D (D stands for *dioptres*). Dioptres tell you how powerful a lens is at converging or diverging light.

Lens power (in dioptres) = $\dfrac{1}{\text{focal length (in metres)}}$

  i) What is the focal length of Lucy's lens?
  ii) Is it a converging or diverging lens? Why?

e) Copy and complete Figure 21 to show what happens to parallel light falling on a lens obliquely.

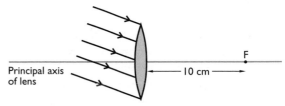

Principal axis of lens

10 cm

F

Figure 21

16 In Figure 22 (see page 74), AB is an illuminated pin in front of a lens of focal length f. The two focal points are marked with an F. The point A is on the principal axis of the lens. Rays of light from B are converged by the lens to a point D. In a similar way, light from point A is converged to point C.

73

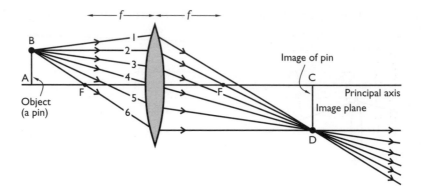

Figure 22

a) What is meant by *principal axis*?

b) Why are there two focal points?

c) In order to locate the image of the whole pin, you have to locate the image of B. The rays from B to the lens have been numbered. You can predict the path of three of these rays. Which are they and where will they go after passing through the lens?

d) Redraw Figure 22, leaving out all except *two* of the rays whose paths you can predict.

e) If you want to see the image of the pin CD, without using a screen, where would you look? (Draw in an eye to show this.)

Optical instruments

Cameras
▶ Light is converged onto light sensitive film.
▶ A camera can have a variable aperture.
▶ Focusing is done by moving the lens, not changing its shape.

The eye
▶ Light from a point on an object enters the eye and converges to a point on the retina. Most of the converging is caused by the cornea.
▶ The shape of the crystalline lens in the eye is changed by the ciliary muscles. This enables the eye to change its focal length for viewing near and distant objects.

▶ The iris controls the amount of light entering the eye.
▶ Short sight (myopia) means that parallel light entering a relaxed eye, converges to a point in front of the retina. Short sight is corrected by wearing spectacles with concave (diverging) lenses.
▶ Long sight (presbyopia) means that parallel light entering a relaxed eye, converges towards a point behind the retina. Long sight is corrected by wearing spectacles with convex (converging) lenses.

Questions

17 Figure 23 shows the main components of a slide projector.

a) Explain the function of the curved mirror and the two condenser lenses.

b) Explain how a picture of the slide is formed on the screen.

c) If the focal length of the projector lens is such that when $x = 10$ cm, $y = 3$ m, what magnification does this produce? (Magnification = image size/object size.)

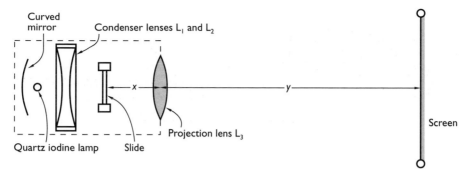

Figure 23

d) Suppose the picture in part (c) is too large to fit on the screen. What two adjustments can be used to remedy this?

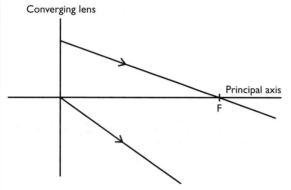

Figure 24

18 a) Figure 24 shows two rays diverging after passing through a converging lens. Copy and complete the diagram to show:
i) using a dotted line, the point from which the rays appear to have come;
ii) using a full line, the point from which the rays have actually come.

b) Part (a) shows the formation of a virtual image. How can it be viewed? (Draw in an eye to show this.)

c) Suppose the object is a pin and the light rays in Figure 24 have come from its head. Describe the virtual image.

19 Alex has been given two lenses, A and B. Lens A has a focal length of 10 cm and lens B one of 5 cm. They both have the same diameter. Explain the answers to the following, using ray diagrams where this helps.

a) Which lens would make a better magnifying glass?

b) Which lens would produce a bigger real image of the Sun?

c) Which lens would be more effective in burning a hole through a piece of card using the Sun's rays?

d) Which lens would you use in a fixed focus camera to get the largest possible picture of a distant view.

20 Figure 25 shows the main features of a camera.

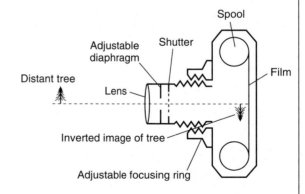

Figure 25

a) Explain the purpose of the following:
i) the adjustable diaphragm;
ii) the shutter;
iii) the adjustable focusing ring.

b) How will reducing the aperture, to let less light into the camera, affect the shape, size, brightness and sharpness of the image formed?

75

c) Wendy has been taking pictures of a distant view, but now wants to take a close up of her friend Jo. To do this she has to adjust the focus to change the lens position. Will the lens have to be moved in, towards the film, or out, away from the film?

d) The brightness of the image is affected by the amount of light let into the camera. Wendy took several pictures on the first day of her holiday when it was sunny, and several more the next day when it was cloudy. What two camera adjustments could Wendy have made to produce pictures of constant brightness?

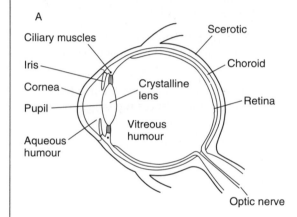

Figure 26

21 Figure 26A shows a section through the human eye. The cornea, aqueous humour and crystalline lens combine to act like a variable focus lens, with air on one side and liquid (the vitreous humour) on the other (Figure 26B).

a) Which part of the eye controls the amount of light entering it?

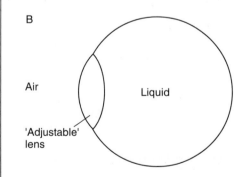

b) How is focusing achieved in the eye?

c) What adjustment is required to keep a car in focus, as it moves towards you?

d) The back of the eye is coated with a light sensitive membrane. What is it called? What is it for?

e) If you compare the eye with a camera, which part of the eye acts like:
(i) the shutter? (ii) the adjustable diaphragm? (iii) the adjustable focusing ring? (iv) the film?

22 A person with normal eyesight can focus on distant objects clearly. Someone with 'short sight' cannot focus distant objects, but can focus close objects.

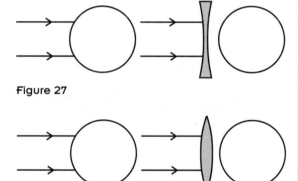

Figure 27

Figure 28

a) David has short sight and has been prescribed glasses with diverging lenses. Copy and complete the diagrams in Figure 27 to show:
i) what happens to parallel light entering David's eye
ii) how diverging lenses can help.

b) Suggest what might cause short sightedness.

c) Graham has long sight and cannot focus on distant or close objects. He requires spectacles with converging lenses to correct his vision. Copy and complete the diagrams in Figure 28 to show:
i) what happens to parallel light entering Graham's eye
ii) how converging lenses might help.

d) Suggest what might cause long sightedness.

9 Electricity

Electrostatics

▶ There are two types of electric charge: positive and negative. Like charges repel; unlike charges attract.

▶ Rubbing one insulating material with another causes charge to separate. One material becomes positive and the other negative.

▶ In an atom the number of positively charged particles in the nucleus balances the number of negatively charged electrons orbiting the nucleus.

▶ If an atom loses electrons it becomes positively charged. If the atom gains electrons it becomes negatively charged. A charged atom, or combination of atoms, is called an ion.

▶ When charges move they produce an electric current.

▶ The presence of ions in gases and liquids enables them to conduct electricity.

▶ In metals, the outer electrons of atoms are detached and are free to move about in the spaces between the atoms. These 'free' electrons enable metal to conduct electricity.

▶ Electrons are emitted from the surface of a hot metal. These electrons can be focused into a beam, and made to travel towards a fluorescent screen, or target.

▶ The beam can be deflected by a pair of oppositely charged parallel plates.

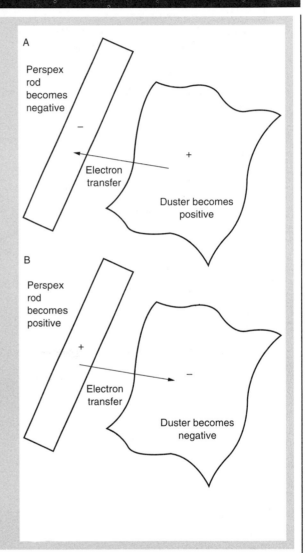

Questions ❔❔❔❔❔❔❔❔❔❔❔❔❔❔❔❔

1 Figure 1A and 1B (see page 78) show simple tests using charged balloons and rods. The rods and balloons have been rubbed vigorously with a duster.

   a) What is the charge on:
       (i) rod X? (ii) rod Y?

   b) What will happen to the two rods if they are suspended side by side (Figure 1C)?

   c) What will happen to the two positively charged balloons if they are suspended side by side (Figure 1D)?

77

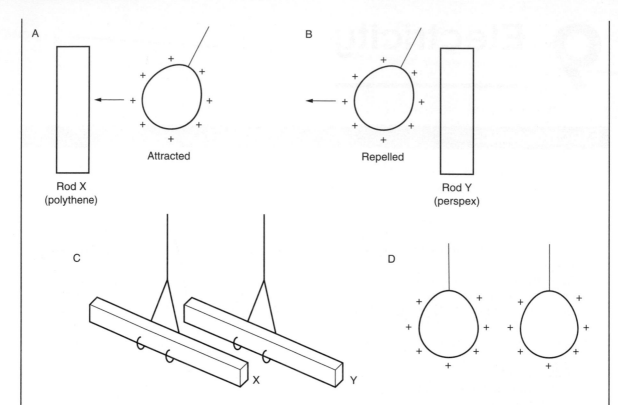

Figure 1

A — Attracted

Rod X (polythene)

B — Repelled

Rod Y (perspex)

C — X, Y

D

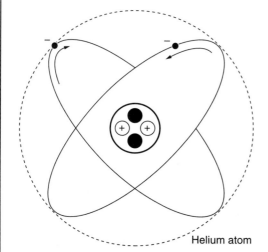

Helium atom

Figure 2

c) How will the total charge on the atom be affected if an electron is removed from it?

d) Suppose an electron were removed from a helium atom, which we shall call A, and became attached to another helium atom, B. What will happen to the charge on B?

e) What is the combined charge on A and B in part (d):
(i) before the event described? (ii) after?

f) Will A and B attract or repel each other?

2 Figure 2 represents a helium atom. The volume of space surrounding the nucleus is vast compared with the volume of the nucleus.

a) Copy the diagram and label each particle and the nucleus.

b) What is the total charge on the helium atom?

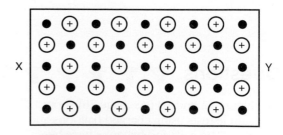

X — Y

⊕ Positively charged parent atom

● Free electron

Figure 3

3 Figure 3 shows some atoms and free electrons in a piece of metal. Each atom has lost about one electron on average. The electrons are free to move about between the parent atoms.

a) Why are the parent atoms positively charged?

b) Where are the electrons which are not free?

c) Redraw Figure 3 to show what happens when a negatively charged rod is held near to end X of the piece of metal. Indicate which end of the metal is positively charged and which negative.

d) Repeat part (c) only this time with a positively charged rod held near end X.

c) What causes electrons to be repelled from the belt onto the dome?

d) The dome becomes highly charged. What is the sign of this charge?

e) Another smaller dome, connected to the base, is held near to the big dome. The smaller dome becomes positively charged. Why?

f) Huge sparks jump across the gap between the two spheres. Explain why this happens.

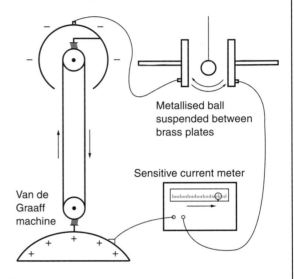

Figure 5

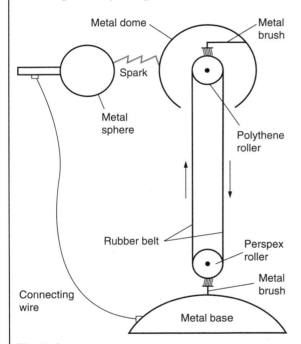

Figure 4

4 Figure 4 shows a model Van de Graaff machine for separating charges. The perspex roller at the bottom is driven by a motor. This causes a rubber belt to revolve, which charges up the two rollers. The perspex becomes positive and the polythene becomes negative.

a) Why are electrons in the metal base attracted towards the perspex roller?

b) What happens to electrons when they reach the belt?

5 Study Figure 5.

a) Suppose you make the ball touch the left hand plate and then release it. Describe and explain the motion of the ball afterwards.

b) Why must the ball have a metallic surface for this to work?

c) The steady reading on the current meter means that there must be movement of electrons through the meter. Write a paragraph to explain how electrons can keep moving round the circuit.

d) Describe and explain what will happen to the meter reading if the plates are moved closer together.

e) The metallised ball acts like a 'charge carrier'. Explain what is meant by this term.

79

Electric circuits

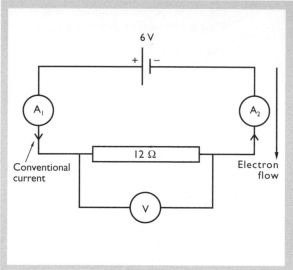

- A battery provides the energy needed to push electrons round an electric circuit.
- The battery voltage (or potential difference) is a measure of the energy given to the electrons. A higher voltage implies more energy.
- Ammeters measure current. A larger current means that more electrons flow per second.
- One amp (1 A) is equivalent to about 1 million, million, million electrons flowing per second.
- Electrons lose energy when they pass through resistors, because they collide with atoms.
- Increasing the resistance in a circuit reduces the current.

Questions

6 Which of the following statements correctly describes the action of a torch battery, when connected to a torch bulb (more than one statement may be correct).

Statement A: The battery can be thought of as a reservoir of electrons, which are stored up, rather like water can be stored in a lake.

Statement B: The battery can be thought of as a provider of energy, which is given to the electrons as they pass through the battery, and lost by electrons as they pass through the bulb.

Statement C: The battery in an electrical circuit can be compared with a pump in a water circuit. Electrons in the wires are forced to move through the wires by the action of the battery, just like water is forced to move through the pipes by the action of the pump.

7 A good way of understanding the flow of electric current along wires is to look at the flow of water along pipes.

a) Write down the rate of flow of water along pipes A and B in Figure 6.

b) Write down the electric current flowing along wires A and B in Figure 7.

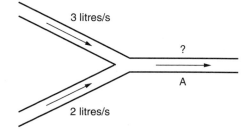

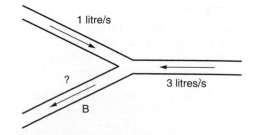

Figure 6

80

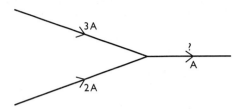

Figure 7

8 Calculate the missing currents in Figure 8. Write down the direction of flow (towards or away from the junction).

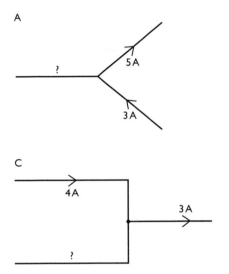

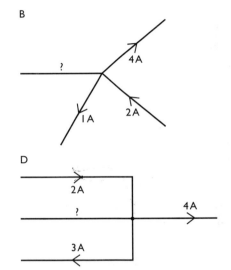

Figure 8

9 Figure 9 shows a combination of SPDT switches, S_1 and S_2, which are used to control bulbs A and B. Copy and complete Table 1 to show which bulb will be **on** and which will be **off**.

Position of S_1	Position of S_2	Bulb A	Bulb B
left	left		
left	right		
right	left		
right	right		

Table 1

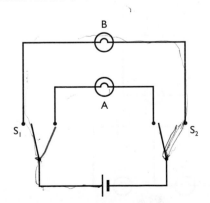

Figure 9

81

In questions 10, 11 and 12 the cells and the bulbs are identical. A **single bulb** connected to a **single cell** glows with **normal brightness**.

10 In Figure 10, state whether bulbs A–H will be brighter or dimmer than normal, normal, or off:

a) when the switches in each circuit are open

b) when the switches in each circuit are closed.

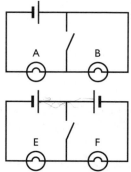

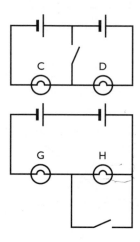

Figure 10

11 Which bulb in Figure 11 will be brighter, or will they be the same:

a) A or B? d) E or F?

b) B or C? e) C or I?

c) A or D? f) J or K?

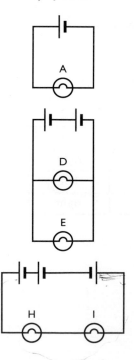

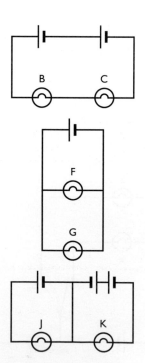

Figure 11

12 In Figure 12, how does the brightness of bulbs A, B and C compare with normal: (i) when the switch is open? (ii) when the switch is closed?
Explain your answers.

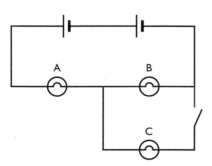

Figure 12

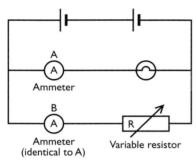

Figure 13

13 Jack and Amanda are trying to measure the resistance of a torch bulb, under working conditions. They use the circuit in Figure 13. R can be changed by 1 ohm (Ω) at a time. The results are shown in Table 2.

Ammeter A (amps)	Ammeter B (amps)	Resistance R (ohms)
0.30	0.37	8
0.30	0.33	9
0.30	0.30	10
0.30	0.27	11
0.30	0.25	12

Table 2

a) Why didn't the readings on ammeter A change?

b) What is the resistance of the bulb? Explain your answer.

c) Amanda argues that it was unnecessary to take all these readings. To prove her point, she selects the readings in the last row of the table and works out the correct value for the bulb's resistance. Explain how she did this.

14 The cells in Figure 14 are identical and maintain constant voltage. The ammeter in Figure 14A reads 1 A, when the resistance is 1 Ω.

a) Calculate the ammeter readings and resistances labelled A_1, A_2, R_1 and R_2 in Figure 14B to 14E.

b) Jack wants to replace two 1 Ω resistors in *series* by a single resistor. What value should it have?

c) Jill wants to replace two 1 Ω resistors in *parallel* by a single resistor. What value should it have?

d) Work out the values of the resistors R_1 and R_2 in Figure 15.

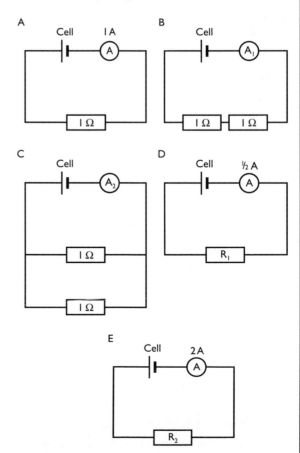

Figure 14

83

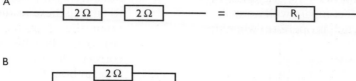
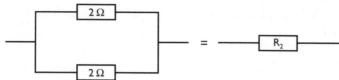

Figure 15

15 Assume all the cells in this question are identical.

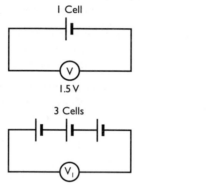
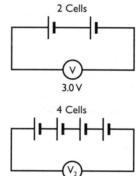

Figure 16

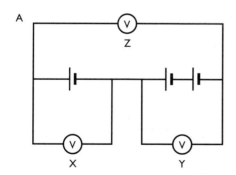
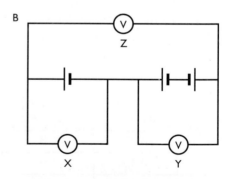
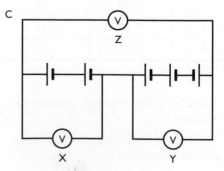

Figure 17

a) What will V_1 and V_2 read (Figure 16)?

b) What will voltmeters X, Y and Z read (Figure 17 A, B and C)?

16 In Figure 18, H_1 and H_2 are battery holders.

A

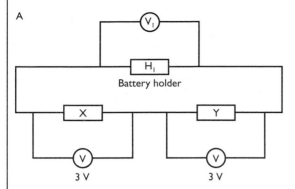

B

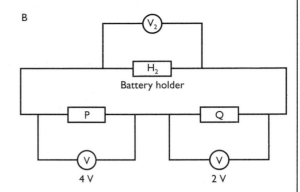

Figure 18

a) What do voltmeters V_1 and V_2 read?

b) How many 1.5 V torch batteries are there in the battery holders H_1 and H_2?

c) How can you tell that resistances X and Y are the same (Figure 18A)?

d) How can you tell that resistances P and Q are different (Figure 18B)? Which is larger?

17 Figure 19 shows *parts* of electric circuits. Some of the values are given, some are not.

a) In Figure 19A, which resistor is greater, A or B? Why?

b) In Figure 19B, which resistor is greater, C or D? Why?

c) In Figure 19C which resistor is the largest, and which the smallest?

18 Jack and Sasha want to check the value of a $10 \ \Omega$ resistor. They draw two circuits (Figure 20), but one of them is wrong.

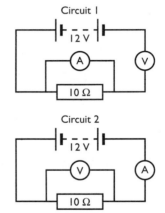

Figure 20

A

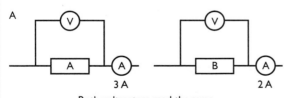

Both voltmeters read the same

B

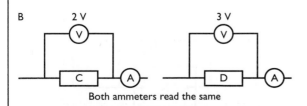

Both ammeters read the same

C

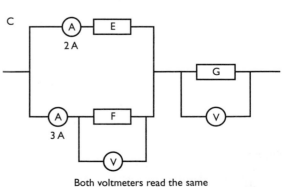

Both voltmeters read the same

Figure 19

85

a) What can you say about the resistance of ammeters and voltmeters?

b) Which instrument is for measuring current?

c) In which circuit are the ammeter and voltmeter correctly connected?

d) What would the ammeter and voltmeter read in each circuit?

e) Explain how to calculate the resistance from the meter readings.

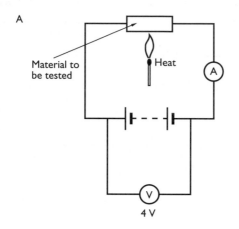

A

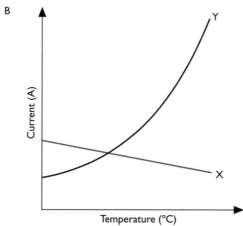

B

Figure 21

19 Alex sets up the circuit in Figure 21A. He wants to find out whether the resistance of various materials changes when heated. Two of the materials under test are: an *iron wire* wrapped round a glass rod, and a *carbon rod*. In a trial experiment, Alex held a match flame under each material. The voltmeter reading remained at 4 V throughout the experiment. The ammeter readings are recorded in Table 3.

	Ammeter reading when cold (A)	Ammeter reading when hot (A)
iron wire	0.4	0.3
carbon rod	0.2	0.8

Table 3

a) Describe how the resistance of the two materials changes when heated.

b) Calculate the resistance of each material when cold.

c) Calculate the resistance of each material when hot.

d) Which material showed the biggest change of resistance when heated?

e) What changes will Alex have to make to the apparatus to measure the temperature of the materials?

f) In another experiment, Alex recorded current and temperature readings and then plotted two lines on a graph (Figure 21B). Which line shows the behaviour of:
(i) the iron wire, (ii) the carbon rod?

g) Both materials can be used to make a resistance thermometer. Give one advantage and one disadvantage of each material.

20 Tara connects up the circuit in Figure 22 to investigate the contents of box X. She knows that it contains one of the following:
- a *light bulb* with a metal filament, whose resistance increases if it gets hot;
- a *carbon thermistor*, whose resistance decreases if it gets hot;
- a *resistor* whose resistance is constant and does not change when heated.

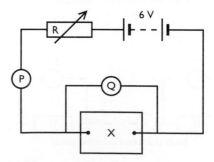

Figure 22

a) Which is the ammeter and which is the voltmeter, P or Q?

b) If the ammeter reads 0.2 A when the voltmeter reads 4 V, what is the resistance of X?

c) The battery is 6 V, the voltmeter reads 4 V, where is the 'missing' 2 V?

d) Calculate the resistance of R.

e) How can Tara increase the current flowing through X, without changing the battery?

f) Sketch a graph of voltmeter readings against ammeter readings for the box containing: (i) the resistor (ii) the light bulb (iii) the thermistor.
Explain the shape of each graph.

Circuit calculations

Quantity	Symbol for quantity	Unit	Symbol for unit
charge	Q	coulomb	C
current	I	ampere	A
potential difference	p.d. or V	volt	V
resistance	R	ohm	Ω
power	P	watt	W
energy	E	joule	J
time	t	second	s

Units and symbols

▶ $\text{Current} = \dfrac{\text{charge}}{\text{time}}$

▶ $\text{Potential difference} = \dfrac{\text{energy}}{\text{charge}}$

▶ $\text{Resistance} = \dfrac{\text{potential difference}}{\text{current}}$

▶ $\text{Power} = \dfrac{\text{energy}}{\text{time}}$

So that:

▶ Electrical Power = potential difference × current

▶ Electrical energy = potential difference × current × time

▶ Customers pay for electrical energy by the kilowatt-hour (kWh).

▶ 1 kWh is equal to the energy used by a 1 kW heater left on for 1 hour.

▶ 1 kWh is equal to 1000 W × 3600 s = 3 600 000 J.

87

Questions ❔ ❔ ❔ ❔ ❔ ❔ ❔ ❔ ❔ ❔ ❔ ❔ ❔ ❔

21 Calculate the missing ammeter or voltmeter readings, or resistances in Figure 23.

a) Find V_1, V_2 and A in Figure 23A.

b) Find V_1, V_2 and A in Figure 23B.

c) Find V_1, V_2 and A in Figure 23C.

d) Find V in Figure 23D.

e) Find R in Figure 23E.

f) Find A and R in Figure 23F.

D

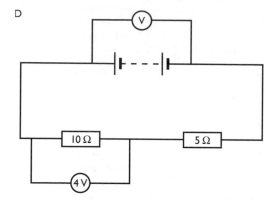

A

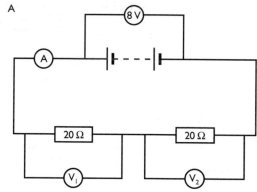

E

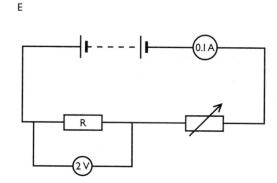

B

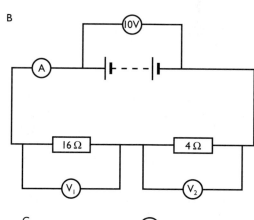

F

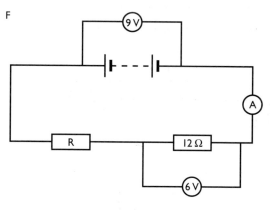

C

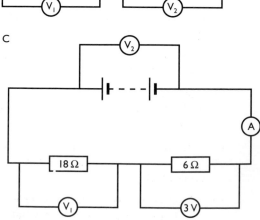

22 Figure 24 shows an experiment to investigate resistance combination. Resistors X and Y can be replaced by a single resistor Z, which has the same effect on the circuit. In this experiment various values of X and Y are chosen (Table 4). Copy and complete Table 4. Calculate the value of Z that would produce the same reading on A_3.

Figure 23

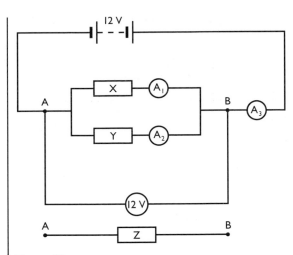

Figure 24

X (Ω)	Y (Ω)	A₁ (A)	A₂ (A)	A₃ (A)	Z (Ω)
6	6				
6	3				
3	6				
12	6				
6	12				
12	4				

Table 4

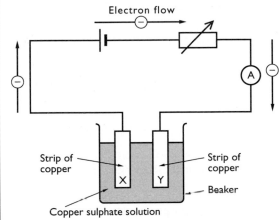

Figure 25

23 Figure 25 shows an electrolysis experiment. A steady current of 0.3 A is passed through a solution of copper sulphate. The copper sulphate contains copper ions (copper atoms which have lost two electrons). When a copper ion picks up **two** electrons, it becomes a copper atom.

a) If the current of 0.3 A is allowed to flow for 1 minute, how many coulombs of charge pass round the circuit?

b) If 1 coulomb is equivalent to about 6×10^{18} electrons, how many electrons pass round the circuit each minute?

c) Are the copper ions positively or negatively charged?

d) On which plate will copper be deposited?

e) How many atoms of copper will be deposited in 1 minute?

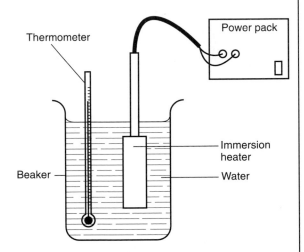

Figure 26

24 Tom carries out an experiment (Figure 26) in which he heats a beaker of water. Tom calculates that 4000 J of electrical energy are supplied to the water in 100 seconds. The current flowing through the heater coil is 4 A.

a) How many coulombs of charge pass through the coil each second?

b) How many coulombs of charge pass through the coil in 100 seconds?

c) How many joules of energy are given to each coulomb of charge by the power pack?

d) Calculate the voltage of the power pack. (*Remember*: a volt is a joule per coulomb.)

e) If Tom connects a voltmeter across the terminals of the power pack, what should it read?

25 a) Calculate the current that each of the following 240 V appliances takes under normal operating conditions:

  i) A 60 W lamp
  ii) A 300 W TV
  iii) A 1 kW microwave oven
  iv) A 900 W toaster
  v) A 3 kW heater

 b) Fuses for use in three-pin plugs are rated 2 A, 3 A, 5 A and 13 A. Decide which fuse should be used for each appliance.

26 A 1.5 V torch battery can maintain a current of 0.3 A for 2 hours. Calculate:

 a) the charge passing round the circuit in this time

 b) the power rating of the battery

 c) the total energy converted by the battery in this time.

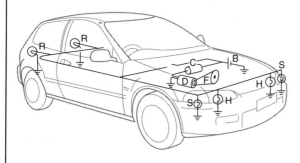

R = Rear lights (5 W)
S = Side lights (5 W)
H = Headlights (60 W)
B = Battery (12 V)

D = Dynamo
C = Cut-out
F = Fan belt
⏚ = Connected to chassis of car

Figure 27

27 Figure 27 shows a simplified wiring diagram for a car. Also in the diagram is the dynamo and cut-out. The switching system is *not* shown in the diagram.

 a) Only **one** wire leads from the battery to the lamps. How does electric current get back to the battery?

 b) What is the advantage of wiring up the light circuit in this way?

 c) Are the bulbs connected in series or in parallel with the battery?

 d) Calculate the power consumption if only the side and rear lights are switched on.

 e) Calculate the power consumption if **all** the lights are on.

 f) The owner turns all the lights on before starting the engine. Calculate the current drawn from the battery. Why is it better to start the engine first?

 g) What stops the battery from discharging through the dynamo when the engine is not running?

 h) When the engine is running, power is provided by the dynamo. Why is it very important to have a tight fan-belt?

 i) The headlamp bulbs are rated at 12 V/60 W. Calculate:
 (i) the current taken by each bulb (ii) the resistance of each bulb, under operating conditions.

28 The cost of electricity is 8p per kWh. In Jane's house, there are six 100 W lights and five 60 W lights.

 a) Calculate the cost of leaving all the lights on for 24 hours.

 b) Calculate how many joules of energy there are in 1 kilowatt hour.

 c) Explain why we prefer to use kilowatt hours rather than joules as a unit.

29 During the school holidays, Tom likes to play computer games. His PC has a power rating of 500 W and he plays games for 3 hours each day. Assume the cost of electricity is 8p per kWh.

 a) How many kWh of energy does Tom's PC require each day?

 b) Calculate how much Tom's hobby will cost his parents by the end of a 6-week holiday.

c) Tom's sister, Mary, watches TV for the same amount of time. The TV has a power rating of 240 W. Calculate the cost of Mary's viewing time.

d) The family argue over the cost of playing computer games and watching TV. Tom and Mary claim that it costs more to mow the lawn and cook meals in 1 week, than playing computer games and watching TV for 6 weeks. Are they right? Use Table 5 to answer this.

Appliance	Power rating (W)	Hours per week in use
lawn mower	720	2
cooker	4800	4
microwave	500	1

Table 5

30 A fan blows air across two heater elements (Figure 28). There are three settings for the fan heater: cold air, warm air or hot air.

a) Complete Table 6, inserting the words **open** or **closed** to indicate how the switches control the three settings.

b) What current passes through each heater element when in use?

c) Which of the following fuses would you choose for the heater, 2 A, 3 A, 5 A or 13 A? Why?

d) 240 V is applied to the connections L and N.
i) What do L and N stand for?
ii) What is the purpose of the connection E?

e) Where in the circuit should the fuse be placed?

f) Although it is possible to have the fan switched on and not the heater elements, it is impossible to have the heater elements switched on and not the fan. Why?

g) Calculate the weekly cost of having the fan heater on for 3 hours each day. (Assume that the cost of electricity is 8p per kWh.)

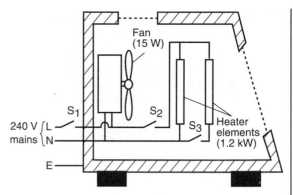

Figure 28

		S_1	S_2	S_3
cold air				
warm air				
hot air				
fan heater and fan off				

Table 6

31 Figure 29 shows two ways of connecting the heating elements in a car rear window. Each element has a resistance of 4 Ω. The points labelled X and Y are connected to the 12 V car battery.

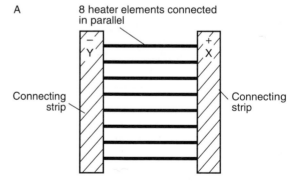

A   8 heater elements connected in parallel

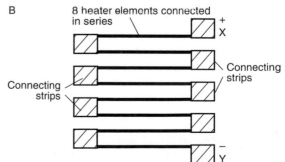

B   8 heater elements connected in series

Figure 29

a) Calculate the current flowing through a single heating element, when connected to 12 V.

b) What is the total current provided by the battery in the parallel arrangement?

c) What is the total current provided by the battery in the series arrangement?

d) Which arrangement will develop the most power?

The cathode ray oscilloscope

▶ In a cathode ray oscilloscope, electrons are emitted from a hot cathode and accelerated towards the anode by a high voltage.

▶ There are two pairs of plates for deflecting the beam vertically or horizontally.

▶ Extra electrodes are used for controlling brightness and for focusing the electron beam.

▶ The CRO tube is evacuated.

▶ A fluorescent screen displays the trace produced by the electron beam as it is deflected to and fro.

▶ A time-base circuit causes the beam to sweep repeatedly across the screen, from left to right, at constant speed.

▶ The CRO can be used to measure voltages, display waveforms, and measure time intervals and frequencies.

Questions ❓ ❓ ❓ ❓ ❓ ❓ ❓ ❓ ❓ ❓ ❓ ❓ ❓ ❓

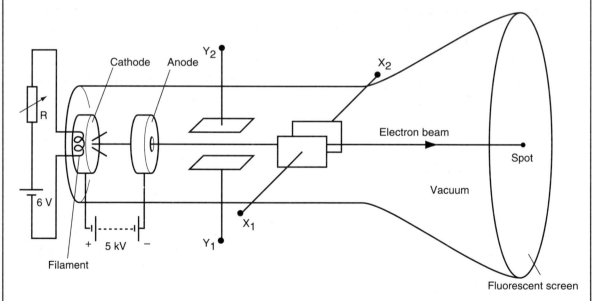

Figure 30

32 Figure 30 shows a simplified diagram of a cathode ray tube. Electrons are emitted from the cathode and attracted towards the anode. They pass through a hole in the anode to form a beam.

a) Describe how the cathode is heated.

b) Explain why you need to heat the cathode.

c) What is the purpose of the 5 kV supply?

d) Why must there be a vacuum in the tube?

e) Why is the inside of the screen coated with fluorescent material?

f) How will the brightness of the spot on the screen be affected by:
   i) increasing the resistance R?
   ii) increasing the voltage between the cathode and the anode?

33 Look again at Figure 30.

a) What is the purpose of the two pairs of parallel plates?

b) Describe what will happen to the beam if:
i) Y_2 is made positive and Y_1 negative
ii) X_2 is made positive and X_1 negative.

c) Explain why the vertical deflection of the spot is slightly greater than the horizontal deflection, when equal voltages are applied to the two pairs of plates.

d) The X and Y plates of an oscilloscope are connected to amplifiers. The amplifiers are designed to make the same voltage applied to the X and Y sockets produce the *same* deflection. What else are the amplifiers designed to do?

34 Figure 31A shows a view of the cathode ray tube screen from in front and the position of the X and Y plates inside the tube. With nothing connected, the spot is central. Figure 31B shows how the spot is deflected when 1 V is connected to the Y sockets and 1 V is connected to the X sockets, making Y_2 and X_2 positive with respect to Y_1 and X_1.

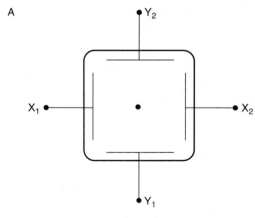

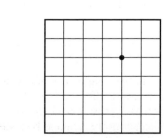

Figure 31

Draw pictures similar to Figure 31B to show what you would see on the screen if:

a) 1 V is connected to the X sockets making X_2 negative with respect to X_1.

b) 2 V are connected to the Y sockets making Y_2 positive with respect to Y_1, and at the same time 1 V is connected to the X sockets making X_2 positive with respect to X_1.

c) An alternating voltage with an amplitude of 2 V is connected to the Y sockets.

d) An alternating voltage with an amplitude of 2 V is connected to the X sockets.

35 An oscilloscope contains additional circuitry. One of the circuits is called a time-base which causes the spot to sweep across the screen, producing a horizontal line. When the spot reaches the end of the line, it is made to fly back to the start and repeat the process. If the time-base is switched on, draw diagrams to show what you would see when carrying out the experiments below:

a) One cell is connected to the Y sockets making Y_2 positive with respect to Y_1.

b) Two cells are connected to the Y sockets making Y_2 negative with respect to Y_1.

c) A low-frequency, alternating voltage is connected to the Y sockets.

d) A high-frequency, alternating voltage is connected to the Y sockets.

36 Figure 32 (see page 94) shows the front of an oscilloscope. Mandy and Tom set the time-base at 0.01 s/cm and the Y amplifier at 5 V/cm. Mandy connects a signal generator to the Y sockets.

a) What is the amplitude of the alternating voltage (AB on the screen)?

b) With the signal generator disconnected, the spot traces a straight line across the screen from C to D. How long does this take?

c) What is the time for one complete oscillation (EF on the screen)?

d) Calculate the frequency of the signal generator (the number of oscillations per second).

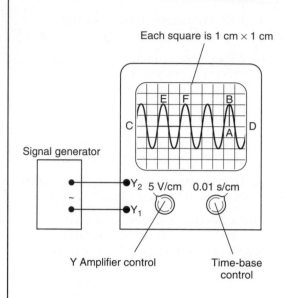

Each square is 1 cm × 1 cm

Signal generator

Y_2 5 V/cm   0.01 s/cm

Y_1

Y Amplifier control   Time-base control

Figure 32

e) Tom changes the Y amplifier setting to 10 V/cm. How will this affect the shape and size of the trace?

f) Mandy changes the Y amplifier back to 5 V/cm but changes the time-base to 0.02 s/cm. Describe the new trace.

37 Figure 33 shows the oscilloscope trace for a time-base of 1 ms/cm and the amplifier at 2 V/cm.

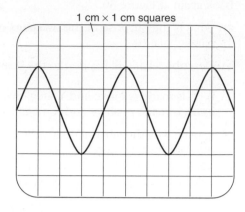

1 cm × 1 cm squares

Figure 33

a) Find the time for one oscillation.

b) Calculate the frequency of the applied voltage.

c) Calculate the amplitude of the applied voltage.

d) Mandy wants to produce five complete oscillations on the screen. What time-base setting is required?

10 Magnets and Electromagnetism

Magnetic fields

▶ A magnetic field is a region in which magnetic forces exist, e.g. near a magnet or near a current-carrying wire.

▶ A magnetic field can be 'mapped' using lines of force to show the magnetic field's direction and strength:

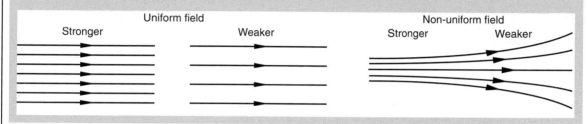

Uniform field — Stronger — Weaker

Non-uniform field — Stronger — Weaker

Questions ？ ？ ？ ？ ？ ？ ？ ？ ？ ？ ？ ？ ？ ？ ？ ？

1 a) Figure 1 shows a bar magnet surrounded by some plotting compasses A, B, C and D. The needle in D points away from the north pole of the magnet. Copy and complete the diagram by drawing in the needles for the other three compasses.

b) Do the same for the compasses in Figure 2.

2 Figure 3A shows a large horseshoe magnet. Figure 3B shows the magnetic field between the poles of the magnet.

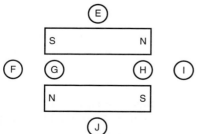

Figure 1

Figure 2

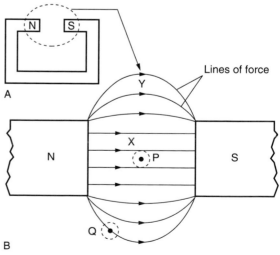

Figure 3

a) Explain what is meant by the term **magnetic field**.

95

b) What does the arrow on a line of force indicate?

c) What does it mean to say that a magnetic field is uniform?

d) Which part of the magnetic field is **uniform**; the region near X or near Y? How can you tell?

e) Sketch Figure 3B (see page 95) and show the directions along which the needles in compasses P and Q point.

f) In which region do you think that the magnetic field is stronger: X or Y?

A

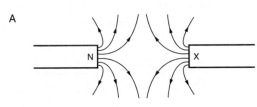

B

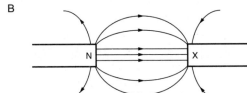

C

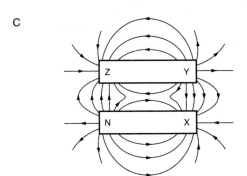

D

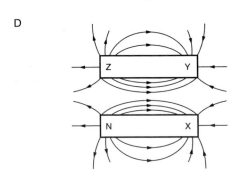

3 In Figure 4 A–D part of the magnetic field between the two magnets has been drawn. Decide which magnets will attract or repel, and which of the poles, marked X, Y and Z, is north (N) or south (S).

A

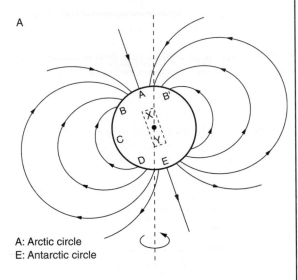

A: Arctic circle
E: Antarctic circle

B

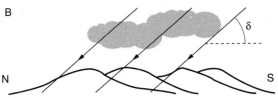

Figure 5

4 The magnetic field around the Earth, looks rather like the field around a bar magnet. We can construct a model Earth by putting a bar magnet inside a small melon. This would allow you to see roughly what the field is like at different points around the globe (Figure 5A).

a) Which way around must you insert the magnet to produce the field lines in Figure 5A; the north end at X or Y?

b) Figure 5B shows the direction of the Earth's magnetic field somewhere on the Earth's surface. Where would you expect the magnetic field to be like this? At A, B, C, D or E?

c) The angle δ in Figure 5B is called the angle of dip. What would you expect the angle of dip to be:
(i) at point C? (ii) at point A?

d) A pocket compass needle does not usually dip down? Why not? How would you hold the compass to see what the angle of dip was?

e) Tom has an idea about using the Earth's magnetic field to propel a ship. He suggests that you magnetise the ship, point the north end of the ship towards the Arctic circle and 'hey presto' the ship moves along a line of force. Explain carefully why this idea won't work.

5 Magnetic fields occur near current-carrying wires. Figure 6A shows an experiment used for plotting the magnetic field near two current-carrying wires. Figure 6B is the same diagram viewed from above.

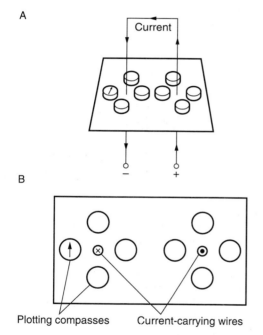

Figure 6

a) What does the cross and the dot tell you about the current direction along the wires?

b) Copy Figure 6B and mark in the correct position of the compass needles. Assume that the magnetic field caused by the wire is much stronger than the Earth's magnetic field.

c) A wire is stretched along a bench top and a compass is placed on top and another underneath the wire (Figure 7A). Assume that the magnetic field around the wire is much stronger than the Earth's magnetic field. Copy Figure 7A and mark in the correct positions of the compass needles.

d) Figure 7B shows the same wire, only this time the magnetic field around the wire is not much stronger than the Earth's field. Copy Figure 7B and mark in the compass needles showing where they point.

e) Figure 7C shows a current-carrying wire on its own, viewed looking along the wire. Draw the magnetic field lines round the wire showing how the magnetic field decreases with distance.

6 Figure 8 (see page 98) shows a long perspex tube with wire wrapped round it to make a solenoid.

a) Copy Figure 8 and mark in the direction that the compass needles 1–5 point when current flows through the wire.

b) Which end of the solenoid acts as a north pole?

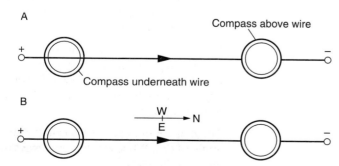

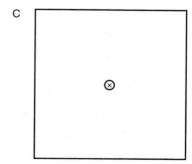

Figure 7

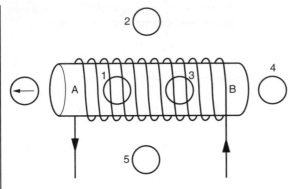

Figure 8

c) Copy the diagram again, leaving out the compasses. Draw magnetic field lines around the solenoid.

d) Suppose you put a steel rod inside the solenoid and make a permanent magnet of the rod. Explain what happens inside the steel rod.

e) If a soft iron rod is placed in the solenoid, it too is magnetised, but not permanently. Explain what this means and how you would show that the iron rod is temporarily magnetised.

Magnetism

▶ Magnet poles are the regions near a magnet from where the field lines appear to diverge, or to where they appear to converge.

▶ In magnetic materials each atom behaves like a miniature magnet. To magnetise these materials you have to align the 'atomic' magnets.

▶ Magnetising can be achieved by placing a magnet near the material, or by placing the material in a solenoid carrying a direct current.

▶ Demagnetising can be done by heating or hammering the material, or by placing it in a solenoid carrying an alternating current, and then slowly withdrawing the material.

▶ Magnetised steel remains magnetised. Soft iron does not. Soft iron can be used to make electromagnets.

Questions

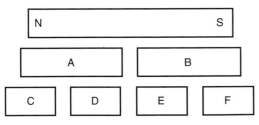

Figure 9

7 Figure 9 shows a bar magnet which has been divided into two equal parts, A and B, and then subdivided into four equal parts, C, D, E and F.

a) Copy Figure 9 and mark in the polarity (N and S) of each part.

b) If you carried on subdividing the bar magnet, you would end up with single atoms. Each atom acts like a tiny magnet. What can you say about the alignment of these atomic magnets in:

i) a magnetised steel rod?

ii) an unmagnetised steel rod?

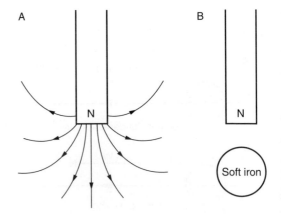

Figure 10

8 a) Figure 10A shows the field lines near the north pole of a bar magnet. Copy Figure 10B and sketch field lines to show how the field is affected by the soft iron ball.

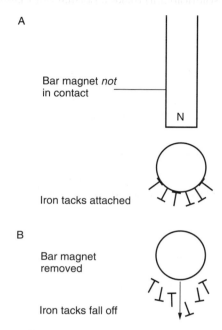

Figure 11

b) Explain why soft iron tacks are attracted to the ball in Figure 11A, but fall off when the magnet is removed (Figure 11B).

9 All elements show some magnetic properties, but only a few show very strong magnetic properties. The best known of these are iron, cobalt and nickel, and several alloys. These elements form strong magnets because the atomic magnets group together to form 'domains'.

a) What does **ferromagnetic** mean?

b) One alloy used to make strong permanent magnets is called Ticonal. Can you guess which elements this contains?

c) What is special about the atoms in a domain?

d) Domains act like small magnets. Using arrows to represent domains, draw diagrams to represent:
i) a magnetised iron bar
ii) an unmagnetised iron bar.

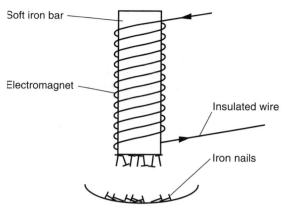

Figure 12

10 Ahmed and Sonja carry out an experiment to test the strength of a simple electromagnet (Figure 12). They use the apparatus to pick up and release small iron nails.

a) Sonja says they ought to use a steel bar instead of an iron bar, because steel is used to make magnets. Is she correct? Explain why.

b) Why must the wire be insulated?

c) Suggest two things Ahmed could do to make the electromagnet pick up more nails.

d) Sonja says that there is a limit to the electromagnet's strength and that it depends on the properties of the iron bar. Is she right? Use domains to explain your answer.

11 Ahmed and Sonja construct a better electromagnet. It consists of a U-shaped iron core with a 'keeper' across the two ends (Figure 13).

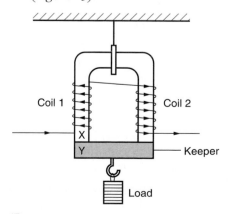

Figure 13

a) What is the polarity of X? What is the polarity of Y?

b) Does it matter if they use D.C. or A.C. current? Explain your answer.

c) How will the strength of the electromagnet be affected by:
i) reversing the windings of coil 1?
ii) reversing the windings of both coil 1 and coil 2?

d) Ahmed finds that when he switches off the current, a light load can still be supported; yet when he removes the keeper he cannot then replace it until the current is switched back on again. Explain why.

Current (A)	0	0.5	1.0	1.5	2.0	2.5	3.0	3.5
Maximum load including keeper (N)	0	2.0	6.0	13.0	21.0	27.0	29.0	29.0

Table 1

12 Ahmed and Sonja produce a table of readings (see Table 1) for the experiment in question 11. They take care doing the experiment because the loads are quite big and there is a tendency for the coils to heat up.

a) Plot a graph of load (y-axis) against current (x-axis).

b) Use your graph to find what current supports a load of 10 N.

c) What effect will the heating up of the iron core have on the results?

d) How can Ahmed and Sonja avoid this overheating?

e) What load could a current of 4.0 A support?

f) Use domain theory to explain the shape of the graph.

Electromagnetism

▶ When a current-carrying wire is placed between the poles of a magnet, the two magnetic fields interact and cause the wire to move. The direction of movement can be worked out using Fleming's left hand rule:

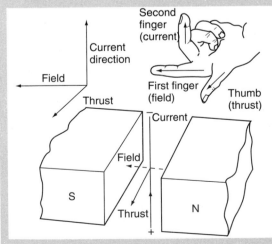

▶ This movement is described as the 'motor effect' and is used to design motors and galvanometers (current measuring instruments).

▶ If a length of wire is moved across a magnetic field, it cuts lines of force, and a voltage is induced in the wire. This voltage can be used to drive a small current round a circuit. This effect is known as the 'dynamo effect', and is used to generate electricity.

▶ Transformers work on the principle that a changing magnetic field will induce a voltage in any coil through which it passes. An alternating current through a primary coil can be used to induce a voltage in a secondary coil.

100

▶ For transformers:

$$\frac{\text{voltage induced in secondary coil}}{\text{voltage applied to primary coil}}$$

$$= \frac{\text{number of turns in secondary coil}}{\text{number of turns in primary coil}}$$

▶ If the transformer is 100% efficient:
power supplied to primary coil = power produced in secondary coil
▶ Electrical power = voltage × current

Questions

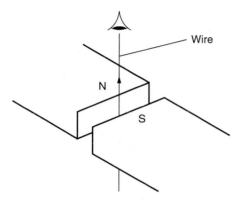

Figure 14

13 When a current flows through the wire in Figure 14, it is forced sideways out of the magnetic field. The questions that follow are designed to help you understand why this happens.

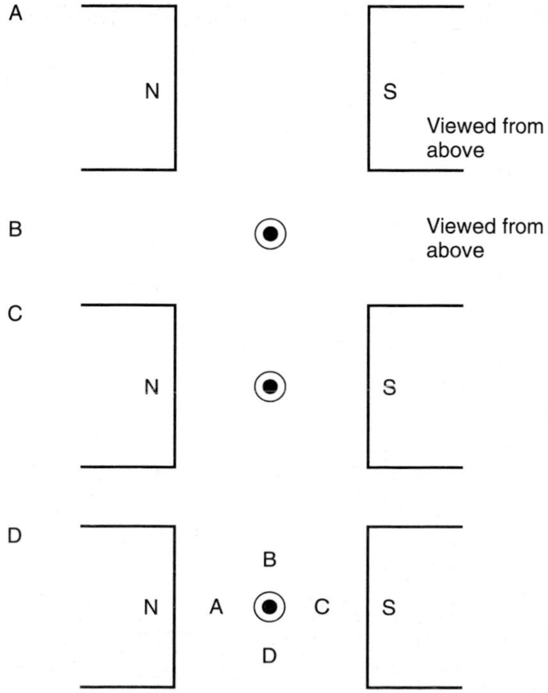

a) Copy Figure 15A and sketch the magnetic field between the poles when there is no wire.

b) Copy Figure 15B and sketch the magnetic field around the current-carrying wire.

c) Copy Figure 15C and sketch the magnetic field that results from the magnetic fields in (a) and (b).

d) Look at your diagram for (c) and at Figure 15D. Where is the magnetic field strongest? Where is it weakest?

e) The magnetic field between the poles of the magnet is distorted by the current-carrying wire. If the tendency of the distorted field is to straighten, which way will the wire be forced to move, towards A, B, C or D?

14 a) Predict the direction of the force acting on the current-carrying wire in Figure 16. Will the force act towards A, B, C, D, E or F? (*Hint:* think about the way the magnetic field between the poles is distorted.)

A

N   S

Viewed from above

B

⊙   Viewed from above

C

N   ⊙   S

D

      B
N   A ⊙ C   S
      D

Figure 15

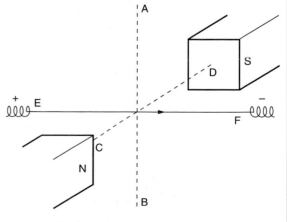

Figure 16

101

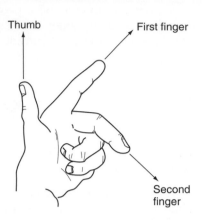

Thumb

First finger

Second
finger

Figure 17

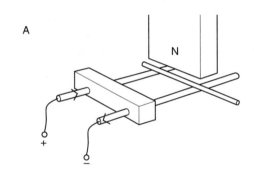

A

N

+ −

15 Figure 19A shows a tightly wound coil held horizontally between the poles of a large magnet. A current flows through the coil. The resulting magnetic field is shown in Figure 19B.

   a) Copy Figure 19B and mark in the forces that act on side AB and side DC of the coil. (*Hint:* use the 'catapult' field idea to help you.)

   b) Will the coil, viewed along XY, try to rotate clockwise or anticlockwise?

   c) Suppose the coil is held vertically between the poles of the magnet (Figure 20). What direction do the forces on sides AB and DC act? Why doesn't the coil rotate in this position?

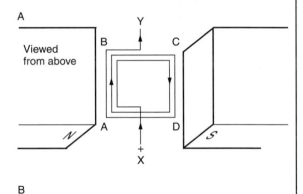

A

Viewed from above

B   Y   C

N   A   D   S

+
X

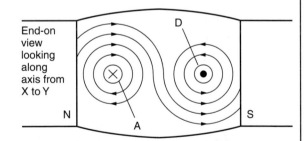

B

End-on view looking along axis from X to Y

D

N   A   S

Figure 19

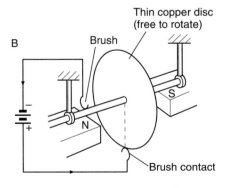

Thin copper disc
(free to rotate)

Brush

B

S

N

Brush contact

Figure 18

   b) Use Flemming's left hand rule (Figure 17), to work out what happens to:
   i) the rod in Figure 18A
   ii) the disc in Figure 18B.

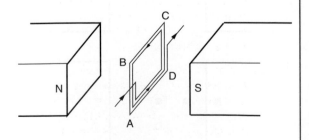

C

B

N   D   S

A

Figure 20

16 Figure 21 shows a model motor. For the position shown in the diagram, the current flows in the direction ABCD.

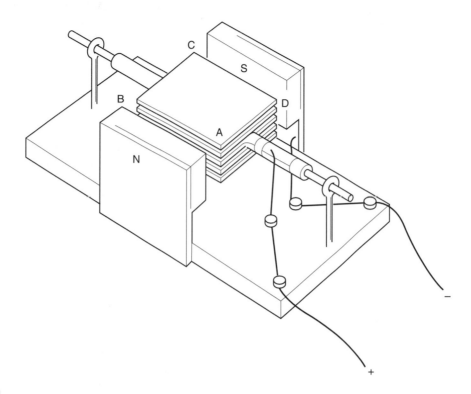

Figure 21

a) Viewed along the spindle (from right to left in the diagram) will the motor rotate clockwise or anticlockwise?

b) Samantha suggests trying out the motor with the brush contacts in a different position. Figure 22A shows how the contacts are positioned in the motor shown in Figure 21. Figure 22B shows another arrangement in which contact is made when the coil is vertical. Will the motor still work? Why?

c) Look again at Figure 22. In which position is the coil most likely to stick? Explain why the coil in fact continues to rotate without sticking.

d) A better arrangement for making contact with the coil is to use a split-ring commutator (Figure 23). Figure 24A–D (see page 104) shows various ways of assembling the motor, its commutator and the magnets. Which arrangements will work and which won't?

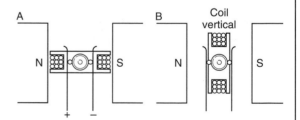

Figure 22

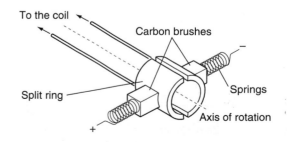

Figure 23

103

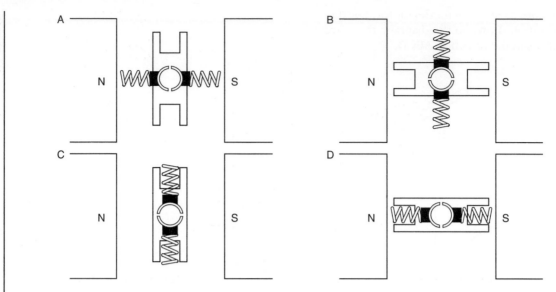

Figure 24

17 Tim and Samantha use a motor kit to construct a model ammeter (Figure 25). They have left out the magnets.

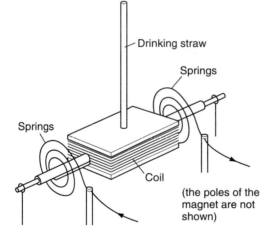

Drinking straw

Springs

Springs

Coil

(the poles of the magnet are not shown)

Figure 25

a) Copy Figure 25 and indicate where the magnets should be placed. Explain how the model ammeter works.

b) Samantha thinks that the ammeter is not very sensitive. Suggest how Samantha could make the ammeter more sensitive.

c) The three diagrams in Figure 26 show a failing in this model: the deflection of the pointer is not *proportional* to the current flowing through the coil.
   i) What does *proportional* mean?
   ii) If the deflection is proportional to the current, what deflection would you expect to get in Figure 26C?
   iii) Assuming the forces acting on each side of the coil are twice as large in Figure 26C as they are in Figure 26B, why don't you get twice the deflection?

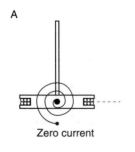

A

Zero current

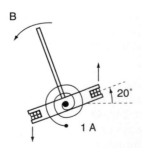

B

20°

1 A

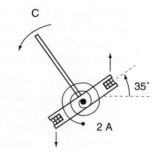

C

35°

2 A

104 | **Figure 26**

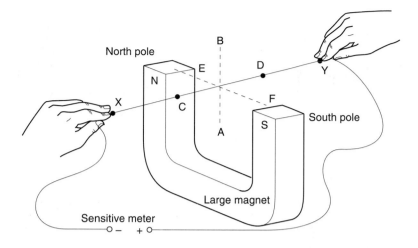

Figure 27

18 Jo and Tamara carry out an experiment which involves moving a length of wire between the poles of a magnet (Figure 27). The wire is connected to a sensitive meter. When the wire cuts across the magnetic field lines, a tiny voltage is induced in it.

a) Whereabouts along the wire is the voltage induced, between X and C, C and D, or D and Y?

b) Which of the following things could Jo do to produce a deflection on the meter:
i) pull the wire towards X, or towards Y?

ii) move the wire sideways towards E, or towards F?
iii) move the wire up towards B, or down towards A?

c) If Jo holds the wire stationary, in which direction must Tamara move the magnet to cause a deflection?

d) Figure 28 A and B show attempts to produce a larger deflection. Will both attempts work, only one or neither? Explain your answer.

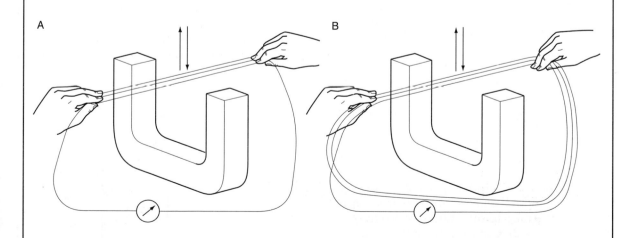

Figure 28

105

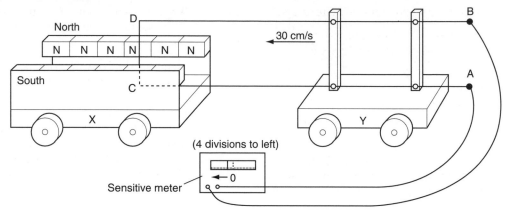

Magnadur magnets
(with poles on each face)

North

N N N N N N

South

C

X

30 cm/s

(4 divisions to left)

Sensitive meter

B

A

Y

Figure 29

19 Figure 29 shows a rather ingenious experiment to illustrate how the voltage induced in a wire depends on its speed across the magnetic field. When trolley X is stationary and trolley Y moves towards it at 30 cm/s, the deflection on the meter is four divisions to the left of zero. Doubling the speed approximately doubles the deflection.

a) In which part of the rectangular wire is the voltage induced?

b) What must CD be doing in order to produce a steady deflection on the meter?

c) If CD remains between the poles of the magnets throughout its motion, state the size of the deflection. Will it be to the left or to the right of zero, in the following situations:
   i) X is stationary and Y moves to the left at 15 cm/s?
   ii) X is stationary and Y moves to the right at 60 cm/s?
   iii) Y is stationary and X moves to the right at 30 cm/s?
   iv) Both X and Y move towards each other, each with a speed of 30 cm/s?
   v) Both X and Y move away from each other, each with a speed of 30 cm/s?
   vi) Both X and Y move in the same direction, each with a speed of 30 cm/s?

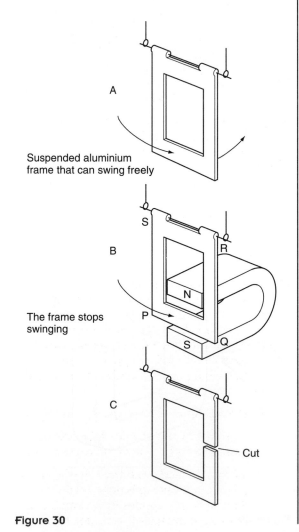

A

Suspended aluminium frame that can swing freely

B

S

R

N

P

The frame stops swinging

S

Q

C

Cut

Figure 30

20 If the frame in Figure 30A is made to swing into a magnetic field (Figure 30B) the swinging stops abruptly.

a) Is aluminium a magnetic material?

b) In which part of the frame will a voltage be induced, when it swings into a magnetic field?

c) If the aluminium frame is cut, as in Figure 30C, it swings freely in the magnetic field. Explain why. Does it matter where the cut is made?

d) Explain why the force acting on the aluminium frame is called an 'opposing force'. When is such a force likely to be set up?

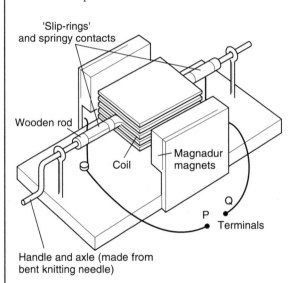

Figure 31

21 Figure 31 shows a model dynamo. By turning the handle, the coil rotates and a small voltage can be generated. Contact to the coil is made by two vertical springy pieces of wire, brushing up against two strips of copper foil, wrapped round the shaft. A centre zero voltmeter is connected to P and Q.

a) Describe how the voltage is induced.

b) Explain why the needle of the voltmeter swings to and fro on either side of zero.

c) When the handle is turned slowly, the amplitude of swing is quite small. Explain what happens to the amplitude of swing if the handle is turned faster.

d) Explain how the amplitude of swing will be affected by increasing the number of turns of wire on the coil?

e) What will happen if one of the magnets is reversed, so that like poles face each other?

f) If the handle is turned very fast, the amplitude of the voltmeter needle becomes very small.
i) Try to explain this effect.
ii) What would you see if P and Q were connected to the Y-plates of a cathode ray oscilloscope with its time-base switched on?

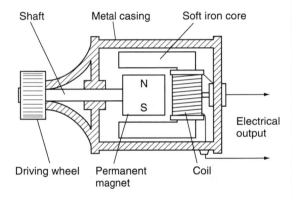

Figure 32

Figure 33

22 Figure 32 shows a bicycle dynamo. It has a rotating magnet and a fixed coil. The output terminals of the dynamo are connected to a cathode ray oscilloscope. Figure 33 A and B show two traces observed on the CRO screen. The setting on the oscilloscope is the same for each trace.

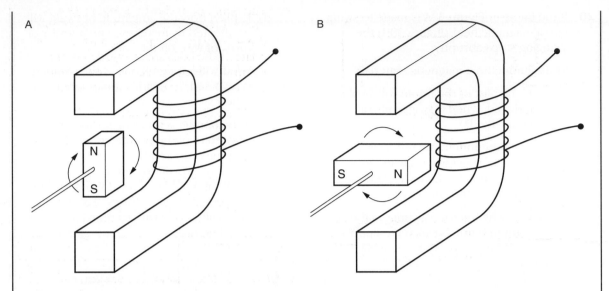

Figure 34

a) Explain why an alternating voltage is produced.

b) If trace A is produced by the dynamo rotating five times each second, at what rate must the dynamo be rotating to produce trace B?

c) Explain why trace B is twice the height of trace A?

d) Figure 34 A and B show two positions of the rotating magnet. Copy trace A, in Figure 33, and mark on it points where the magnet is:
i) passing through the vertical, as in Figure 34A
ii) passing through the horizontal, as in Figure 34B.

e) Try to explain the shape of the trace.

23 In Figure 35 the ends of a long wire are connected to a bulb to make a large loop. The wire is slowly wound round a soft iron C-core on which there is a 500-turn coil connected to the 240 V mains. After winding about five turns of wire round the core, the bulb begins to glow; after another five turns it glows brightly.

a) What causes the bulb to light?

b) Why do more turns make the bulb brighter?

c) What would happen if an iron bridge was placed across the top of the C-core?

24 Dominic makes a model transformer by joining together two C-cores and using two wire coils (Figure 36).

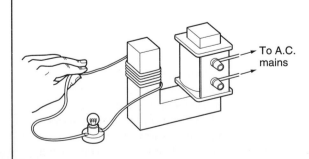

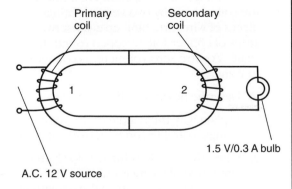

Figure 35

Figure 36

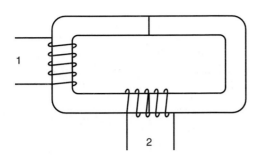

Figure 37

a) Explain how electrical power is transferred from the primary coil to the secondary coil.

b) Why doesn't this arrangement work if a 12 V D.C. source is used?

c) Does it matter where you place the secondary coil e.g. Figure 37?

d) If the bulb lights with normal brightness, how much power is transferred?

e) What current must be flowing in the primary circuit?

25 The equipment shown in Figure 38 was set up to show how the primary voltage and the secondary voltage in a transformer are related. The coils are changed and the voltmeter readings recorded each time (Table 2). Some readings are missing.

a) Study the results in the first two columns of Table 2 and then work out the missing readings in the remaining four columns.

b) Find an expression relating V_1, V_2, n_1, and n_2 in the form $\dfrac{V_1}{V_2} = ?$

V_1	12	12	20	?	8	240
V_2	3	60	80	12	?	12
n_1	1000	1000	?	1200	500	1000
n_2	250	5000	1000	400	2000	?

Table 2

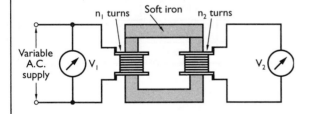

Figure 38

109

11 Control

Cells, switches and resistors

Questions ❓❓❓❓❓❓❓❓❓❓❓❓❓❓

The first part of this chapter requires knowledge of switches, diodes, resistors, light dependent resistors (LDRs) and thermistors. The resistance of an LDR is high in the dark but low in bright light: the resistance of a thermistor is low when it is warm and high when it is cold.

1 a) Which indicators will light in Figure 1 when:
   i) switches S_2 and S_3 only are closed?
   ii) switches S_1 and S_2 only are closed?

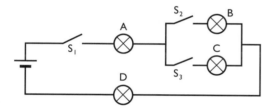

Figure 1

   b) Which indicators will light in Figure 2 when S_4, S_5 and S_6 are closed?

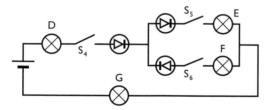

Figure 2

2 You have a cell, an indicator lamp, L, and three switches S_1, S_2 and S_3.

   a) Draw a circuit so that L will light when S_1, S_2 and S_3 are all closed.

   b) Draw a circuit so that L will light when S_1 or S_2 or S_3 is closed.

   c) Draw a circuit so that L will light when S_1 and either S_2 or S_3 are closed.

3 a) Table 1 below can be used to describe the state of the indicator lamp in Figure 3. Copy and complete the table. Remember that closing a switch here shorts out the cell.

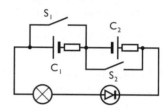

Figure 3

Switches		Lamp (on/off)
S_1	S_2	
open	open	
open	closed	
closed	open	
closed	closed	

Table 1

   b) Draw another table to show the state of the lamp if
   i) the diode is reversed
   ii) the diode is removed.

   c) Draw a third table to show the state of the indicator if C_1 and S_1 are removed.

4 Copy and complete Table 2 to show how temperature and light intensity affect the two LEDs in Figures 4 and 5.

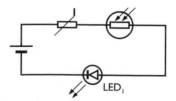

Figure 4

110

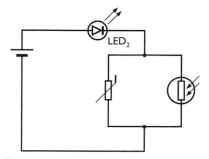

Figure 5

Conditions	LED₁	LED₂
hot, dark		
hot, light		
cold, dark		
cold, light		

Table 2

Transistors, gates, relays, potential dividers

▶ A small current in a coil sets up a magnetic field which closes a switch. The closing of a switch can turn on a larger current.

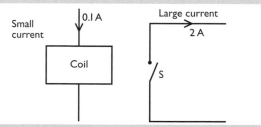

Figure 6 Relay

▶ A transistor is an electronic switch, which can be turned on or off 1000 million times per second. A small current e.g. 1 mA going into the transistor's base (B) can switch on or off a larger current e.g. 100 mA going into the collector (C).

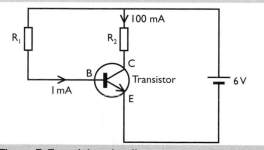

Figure 7 Transistor circuit

▶ For the potential divider here the ratio of the voltages equals the ratio of resistances.

$$\frac{V_1}{V_2} = \frac{R_1}{R_2}$$

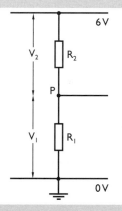

Figure 8 Potential divider

▶ Transistors can be linked into integrated circuits to make NOT, NOR, OR, AND, NAND gates.

Questions

5 In this question refer to the potential divider in Figure 8 above. The voltage at P is 'high' if it is above 3 V, and the voltage at P is 'low' if it is 3 V or below. Copy and complete Table 3 on page 112.

111

R₁ (Ω)	R₂ (Ω)	State of P
100	500	
3	30	
1000	500	
10 000	10	
100	100 000	
200	2000	

Table 3

6 Calculate the voltage at P in Figure 8 on page 111 when
   i) $R_2 = 5\,k\Omega$, $R_1 = 1\,k\Omega$
   ii) $R_2 = 3\,k\Omega$, $R_1 = 3\,k\Omega$
   iii) $R_2 = 2\,k\Omega$, $R_1 = 10\,k\Omega$
   iv) $R_2 = 15\,k\Omega$, $R_1 = 45\,k\Omega$

7 a) Describe the action of a relay.

   b) Describe the action of a transistor.

   c) What advantages does a transistor have over a relay?

   d) What advantage does a relay sometimes have over a transistor?

8 Draw circuit symbols and truth tables for each of the following gates: AND, NAND, NOT, NOR, OR.

9 The circuit in Figure 9 includes a fixed resistor, R, a light dependent resistor (LDR), a light emitting diode (LED), and a logic gate, G.

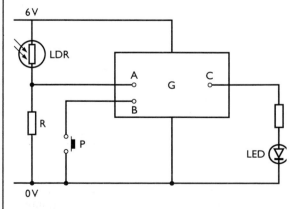

Figure 9

   a) Which parts of the circuit correspond to
      i) the input stage?
      ii) the process stage?
      iii) the output stage?

The LED glows during the day, but goes out if P is pressed. At night the LED does not glow whether P is pressed or not.

   b) i) Make a truth table to show the states of A, B and C. B is high unless P is pressed.
      ii) What sort of logic gate is G?

   c) The LDR and fixed resistor are swapped over. Describe the action of the circuit now.

   d) Design a circuit to make an LED come on automatically in cold weather.

10 Figure 10 shows a circuit which might be used to keep a greenhouse watered while the owner is away on holiday.

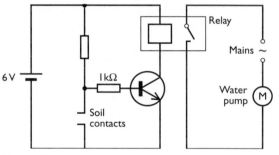

Figure 10

   a) Explain how the circuit detects that the soil is too dry.

   b) Explain why both a transistor and a relay are needed to operate the water pump.

   c) Why does the pump switch off, when the soil has been watered? This is an example of negative feedback; explain why.

11 The circuit in Figure 11 is designed to turn on a greenhouse heater if it gets too cold.

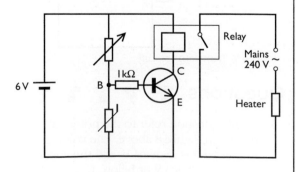

Figure 11

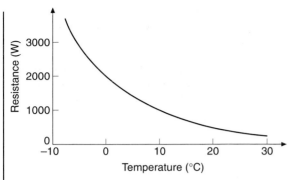

Figure 12

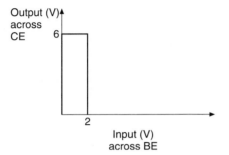

Figure 13

a) Explain how the circuit works

The variable resistor is set to a value of $4\,k\Omega$. Figure 12 shows how the resistance of the thermistor depends on temperature. Figure 13 shows how the output voltage of the transistor across CE depends on the input voltage across BE.

b) Use the information in Figures 11, 12 and 13 to work out the temperature at which the heater turns on.

c) What value must the variable resistor be adjusted to, so that the heater turns on at $10\,°C$?

d) Design a circuit so that a fan turns on to cool the greenhouse down, if the temperature rises above $20\,°C$. State what value of resistors you would use.

12 Table 4 is the truth table for an AND gate.

A	B	Output
0	0	0
0	1	0
1	0	0
1	1	1

Table 4

a) Use Table 4 to explain why the buzzer sounds in Figure 14 when it is light *and* warm.

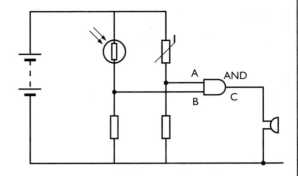

Figure 14

b) Design a circuit to make the buzzer sound if it is
i) dark *and* cold
ii) light *and* cold.

13 a) Explain the operation of a capacitor.

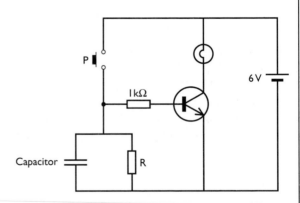

Figure 15

b) In Figure 15, when P is pressed and released the light bulb turns on for 3 seconds and then goes out again. Explain why.

c) What change would you make so that the light stays on for 6 seconds?

d) Draw a circuit (similar to Figure 15), including a relay, so that you could make a mains bulb in your house stay on for 6 seconds when P is pressed.

14 The inputs to the NAND gates in Figure 16 (see page 114) automatically go high unless they are held low. At the moment the LED is off.

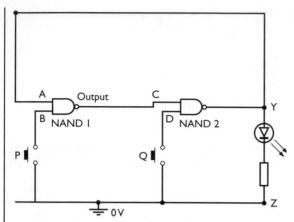

Figure 16

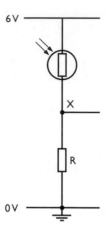

Figure 17

a) What is the voltage state of
   (i) Y   (ii) Z?

b) When Q is pressed the LED turns on, and stays on. Explain why.

c) How would you turn the LED off again?

d) Explain how this latch could be useful in designing a burglar alarm.

15 Figure 17 shows a light dependent resistor, LDR, in series with a fixed resistor, R. A bright light is shining onto the LDR.

a) i) Is the voltage at X high or low? Explain your answer.
   ii) What happens to the voltage at X when the LDR is covered up?

b) Redraw Figure 16, including an LDR and fixed resistor, so that the LED between Y and Z is turned on when a burglar crosses the light beam falling onto the LDR.

c) A friend suggests putting a buzzer between Y and Z to signal when a burglar arrives.
   i) Explain why the buzzer might not work.
   ii) Explain how the circuit might be adapted to make the buzzer work.

16 a) Draw a circuit to show how two NAND gates can be joined to make a bistable.

b) Explain how this bistable stores one piece of information, and how many bistables can be used as an electronic memory.

12 Radioactivity and the Nucleus

The nucleus

▶ The diameter of an atom's nucleus is about 100 000 times smaller than the diameter of the whole atom.

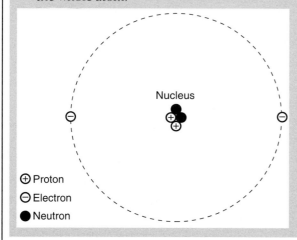

⊕ Proton
⊖ Electron
● Neutron

▶ The nucleus contains protons and neutrons only.
▶ Electrons move round the nucleus.
▶ **Protons** have 1 unit of positive charge and 1 unit of mass.
▶ **Neutrons** have no charge and 1 unit of mass.
▶ **Electrons** have 1 unit of negative charge and a negligible mass.
▶ Atoms have the **same** number of protons and electrons so are electrically neutral.
▶ A nucleus is described by a proton number and a nucleon number. A nucleon is either a proton or neutron. Helium is shown as ^4_2He. It has 2 protons and 4 nucleons (2 protons and 2 neutrons).

Questions

1 Which of these particles – proton, neutron, electron – exist in the nucleus of an atom?

2 What is a nucleon?

3 What is (i) the proton number of a nucleus; (ii) the nucleon number of a nucleus?

4 How many protons and neutrons are there in each of the following nuclei?

a) $^{205}_{81}\text{Tl}$ b) $^{109}_{47}\text{Ag}$ c) $^{107}_{47}\text{Ag}$

d) $^{259}_{102}\text{No}$ e) $^{160}_{66}\text{Dy}$ f) $^{160}_{64}\text{Gd}$

Properties of radiation

▶ Some atoms have unstable nuclei. These can emit radiations to produce more stable atoms. There are three types of radiation: alpha (α), beta (β) and gamma (γ).
▶ An alpha particle is a helium nucleus. It causes strong ionisation, and travels 5 cm in air. It is stopped by a sheet of paper.
▶ A beta particle is a fast moving electron. It causes a lot less ionisation than an alpha

particle, travels several metres in air, and is stopped by thick plastic or thin sheets (2 mm thick) of aluminium or other metals.
▶ Gamma rays are short wavelength electromagnetic waves. These are weakly ionising; they travel great distances and the intensity of radiation can only be reduced (not stopped entirely) by thick sheets of lead.

Questions ❓ ❓ ❓ ❓ ❓ ❓ ❓ ❓ ❓ ❓ ❓ ❓ ❓ ❓

5 You are presented with three radioactive sources. You are told that one of them is an alpha source, one is a beta source and the third is a gamma source. Explain carefully how you might tell them apart.

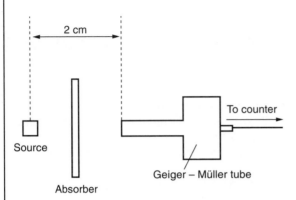

Figure 1

6 You are presented with two sources, X and Y. These sources might emit more than one type of radiation. Each source is placed in front of a Geiger–Müller tube, and then various absorbers are placed in front of the source (Figure 1). Tables 1 and 2 show the counts taken over a 100-second period. Work out which radiations are emitted by each source. (When there is no source the count is 20.)

Absorber	Averaged count
none	5100
paper	3200
aluminium (5 mm thick)	3200
lead	600

Table 1 Source X

Absorber	Averaged count
none	2300
paper	1700
aluminium (5 mm thick)	20
lead	20

Table 2 Source Y

7 Figure 2 shows a spark counter. When a radioactive source is brought near, sparks are produced in the gap between the gauze and the wire.

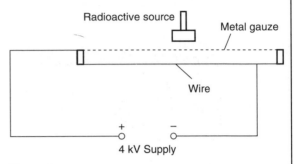

Figure 2

a) Which type(s) of radiation will produce these sparks?

b) Explain what the radiation does to produce the sparks.

c) The source is moved about 5 cm above the gauze and the sparking stops. Explain why.

8 Figure 3 shows some tracks in a cloud chamber.

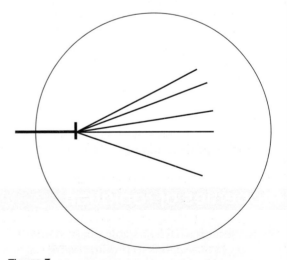

Figure 3

a) How are the tracks produced?

b) Which type of radiation caused them?

c) The source is replaced by a weaker source of the same material. What will happen to the tracks?

9 a) An alpha source is held near to a positively charged electroscope (Figure 4). The leaf falls. Explain why.

b) A lighted match can also be used to discharge the electroscope. Explain why.

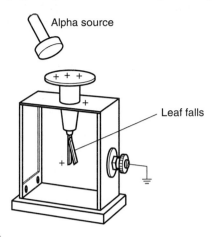

Alpha source

Leaf falls

Figure 4

Radioactive hazards

- Very high doses of radiation can have the same effect as a burn.
- Lower doses cause damage because radiation causes **ionisation**. Ions in the body can produce acids which attack and alter your cells. This can cause cancer.
- If you swallow or inhale an alpha source, it will cause the most damage because it is the most strongly ionising radiation.
- A gamma source outside the body is more dangerous than an alpha source, because the gamma rays can penetrate you.

- We are always exposed to some radiation from our surroundings. This radiation is emitted by rocks, bricks in buildings, the Sun, even the food we eat. This is called background radiation. The background count varies from place to place. It is greater in regions with exposed granite rock e.g. Cornwall.
- A radioactive source has a half-life. If the source has a half-life of 2 hours, it means that half the material has decayed after 2 hours. In the next 2 hours a further half decays and so on.

Questions

10 a) Why must a radioactive source be handled with long tongs?

b) In hospitals strong sources of radiation are handled by remote control, with the operator watching through a thick screen. Why?

c) Why are people under 16 not allowed to handle radioactive materials?

11 After the Chernobyl reactor disaster, some sheep in the UK were affected by radioactive fall-out. People were advised not to eat them.

a) What is **radioactive fall-out**?

b) How did the radioactive material reach the UK?

c) Why were people advised not to eat the sheep?

d) Which is more dangerous to eat, a sheep contaminated with a radioactive source emitting (i) alpha radiation or (ii) gamma radiation? Explain your answer.

12 Your teacher shows you some experiments in class using two sources, an alpha source and a gamma source. You are sitting at the back of the class. Explain which source is more dangerous to you.

13 Table 3 shows some data for groups of workers who have been exposed to various types of radiation. Use the table to make some conclusions about the relative dangers of alpha and gamma radiation. Use your knowledge of these types of radiation to comment on your conclusion.

Source of radiation	Type of radiation	Number of people studied	Extra deaths from cancer caused by radiation
uranium miners	alpha	3400	60
radium luminisers	alpha	800	50
medical treatment	X-rays†	14 000	25
Nagasaki bomb	gamma rays	7000	20

Table 3

† X-rays have a similar effect on humans to gamma rays

Radioactive decay

- When a nucleus emits an alpha or beta particle it changes into a daughter nucleus. A gamma ray takes away energy but otherwise does not alter the nucleus.
- An example of alpha decay:
$$^{213}_{84}\text{Po} \rightarrow ^{209}_{82}\text{Pb} + ^{4}_{2}\text{He}$$
The alpha particle takes away 4 units of mass and 2 units of charge.

- An example of beta decay:
$$^{225}_{88}\text{Ra} \rightarrow ^{225}_{89}\text{Ac} + ^{0}_{-1}\text{e}$$
The electron (beta particle) is emitted from the radium nucleus; a neutron is turned into a proton.
- $^{235}_{92}\text{U}$ and $^{237}_{92}\text{U}$ are both **isotopes** of uranium. They are the same element because they each have 92 protons; U-237 has 2 extra neutrons.
- Isotopes behave the same chemically; but they have different masses.

Questions ❓ ❓ ❓ ❓ ❓ ❓ ❓ ❓ ❓ ❓ ❓ ❓ ❓ ❓

14 Copy and complete the following examples of radioactive decay to include the nucleon and proton numbers of the daughter nucleus.

a) $^{137}_{55}\text{Cs} \rightarrow \quad \text{Ba} + ^{0}_{-1}\beta$

b) $^{133}_{54}\text{Xe} \rightarrow \quad \text{Cs} + ^{0}_{-1}\beta$

c) $^{199}_{80}\text{Hg} \rightarrow \quad \text{Hg} + ^{0}_{0}\gamma$

d) $^{257}_{100}\text{Fm} \rightarrow \quad \text{Cf} + ^{4}_{2}\alpha$

e) $^{241}_{95}\text{Am} \rightarrow \quad \text{Np} + ^{4}_{2}\alpha$

15 $^{240}_{93}\text{Np}$ (neptunium) decays to $^{228}_{89}\text{Ac}$ (actinium), by a series of emissions of alpha and beta particles. How many alpha and how many beta particles are emitted?

16 It has been suggested that some nuclei might decay by a process of double beta decay; this means emitting two beta particles simultaneously. An example is given below. Copy and complete the equation to include the missing nucleon and proton numbers.

$$^{82}_{34}\text{Se} \rightarrow \quad \text{Kr} + ^{0}_{-1}\beta + ^{0}_{-1}\beta$$

17 The isotope of uranium $^{238}_{92}\text{U}$ is found in some rocks. This isotope decays to produce the stable isotope $^{206}_{82}\text{Pb}$ (lead).

a) How many alpha particles are emitted in this decay chain?

b) Have any other particles been emitted too?

c) How does radioactivity cause rocks to warm up?

18 In an experiment involving a radioactive source, a Geiger–Müller tube and a counter, the readings in Table 4 were obtained. The average background count was 20 counts per minute.

Time (hours)	0	1	2	3	4	5	6	7
Counts per minute	930	680	500	370	280	210	160	120

Table 4

a) Draw a table to show the corrected count rate.

b) Plot a graph of corrected counts per minute (y-axis) against time (x-axis).

c) Work out the half-life of the source.

19 A sample of the radioisotope xenon-133, mass 40 g, is delivered to a hospital for use at 9.00 am on 3rd May. The half-life of the isotope is 5 days.

a) What is meant by the term **radioisotope**?

b) How much xenon will be left at 9.00 am on 18th May?

20 Wood contains a lot of carbon, most of which is the isotope $^{12}_{6}C$. There is also a small fraction of the radioactive isotope $^{14}_{6}C$. This isotope decays to $^{14}_{7}N$, with a half-life of about 6000 years. While a tree is alive it contains a constant fraction of carbon-14, but after the tree dies this fraction decreases because of radioactive decay. Measurement of this fraction allows us to work out the age of prehistoric wood.

a) What is an isotope?

b) What is the difference between $^{14}_{6}C$ and $^{12}_{6}C$?

c) What particle does $^{14}_{6}C$ emit when it decays?

d) An archaeologist collects a sample of prehistoric wood and compares it with an equal mass of living wood. The prehistoric wood was found to have a decay rate of 30 disintegrations per hour, while the living wood produced 120 disintegrations per hour.
i) Estimate the age of the prehistoric wood.
ii) Give a reason why this method of dating is not very accurate.

21 Table 5 below shows information about some radioactive isotopes.

a) You are a medical physicist working in a hospital. Advise the consultants which isotopes are suitable for the following tasks.
i) Checking for a blockage in a patient's lungs.
ii) Directing a strong dose of radiation deep into a patient to treat cancer.

Explain in each case what apparatus you would use, explain why you have chosen a particular isotope and what safety precautions you would take to protect the doctors and the patient.

Isotope	Solid, liquid or gas at 20 °C	Type of radiation	Half-life
hydrogen-3	gas	beta	12 years
cobalt-60	solid	gamma	5 years
strontium-90	solid	beta	28 years
xenon-133	gas	gamma	5 days
terbium-160	solid	beta	72 days
actinium-227	solid	alpha	22 years
americium-241	solid	alpha	430 years

Table 5

b) A company makes plastic sheeting by rolling it out between rollers. Two problems arise: (i) they need to check that the sheet is of uniform thickness; (ii) the sheet gets charged and needs to be discharged.

Choose two isotopes to help solve these problems. Explain your choice and how the problems will be solved. What safety regulations would you enforce?

22 a) What is the name of the process which produces energy in the Sun?

b) What is the process called which produces energy in nuclear power stations?

c) Briefly explain what happens in each of these processes.

23 Uranium occurs naturally. Its two most *abundant* isotopes are $^{238}_{92}U$ (99.3%) and $^{235}_{92}U$ (0.7%). Uranium-235 can absorb a slow moving neutron, which causes its nucleus to undergo *spontaneous fission*. A nuclear power station is fuelled by *enriched fuel rods*, which contain 97% of uranium-238 and 3% of uranium-235. This enables a *chain reaction* to occur. The process is helped by a *moderator*. In the event of an emergency the power station can be shut down using boron control rods. Energy produced in the core of the nuclear reactor is used for the generation of electricity.

a) Explain carefully each of the words and phrases in italics in the paragraph above.

b) Why are boron control rods necessary? How do they work?

c) Explain how electricity is generated in a nuclear power station. Mention the energy changes which occur.

d) Give two reasons for using nuclear power, and two reasons for not using it.

13 Earth and Atmosphere

▶ We use a set of symbols to describe the weather.

Wind speed

Strength	Symbol	Speed in knots	Beaufort scale
Calm	◉	0	0
Light breeze		5	2
Gentle breeze		10	3
Fresh breeze		20	5
Gale		35	8
Storm		50	10

Cloud cover

Clear, 1/8, 2/8, 3/8, 4/8, 5/8, 6/8, 7/8, 8/8

Weather

⸲ Drizzle		△ Hail	
● Rain		≡ Fog	
▽ Showers		= Mist	
✳ Snow		ⵕ Thunder	

▶ A weather station model is used to describe the weather in one place.

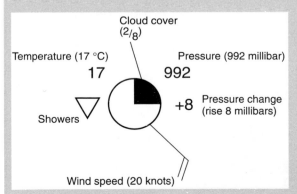

Cloud cover (2/8)
Temperature (17 °C) — 17
Pressure (992 millibar) — 992
+8 Pressure change (rise 8 millibars)
Showers ▽
Wind speed (20 knots)

A weather station model (the writing is there to help you in this example).

▶ The weather in Britain is controlled by five main air masses. When the air flows over the sea it picks up moisture. Continental air masses are drier.

▶ The Earth is warmed more by the Sun's radiation at the Equator than at the poles. Heat is transferred by convection currents in the atmosphere and oceans, from the Equator towards the poles.

121

Questions ❓❓❓❓❓❓❓❓❓❓❓❓❓❓❓❓

1 Three weather station models are shown for weather stations A, B and C for 13.00 hours today. Describe the weather at each point (Figure 1).

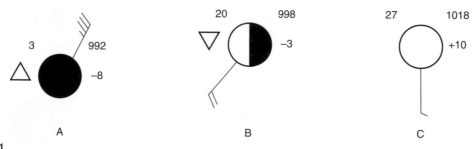

Figure 1

2 At 18.00 hours yesterday the weather at stations A, B and C was described as follows. In each case draw a station model.

Station A

pressure: 1004 mb
pressure change: rise of 3 mb
temperature: 7 °C

cloud cover: $\dfrac{7}{8}$

wind: 20 knots from east
rain

Station B

pressure: 1005 mb
pressure change: drop of 2 mb
temperature: 22 °C

cloud cover: $\dfrac{3}{8}$

wind: 10 knots from east
drizzle

Station C

pressure: 1020 mb
pressure change: no change
temperature: 33 °C
cloud cover: clear
wind: calm

3 Figure 2 shows five main air masses which affect the weather in the British Isles.

Figure 2

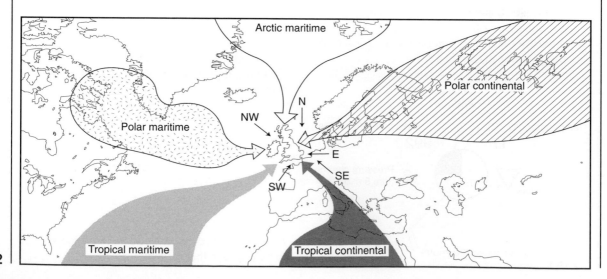

a) Summarise the sort of weather which each air mass brings to us.

b) Polar and tropical maritime air masses affect Britain for over half the year. Use this fact to explain why the annual rainfall on the west of Ireland is on average three times the average rainfall in the south-east of England.

c) Why is tropical maritime air more likely to bring heavy rain than Arctic maritime air?

d) Which air mass is likely to bring
   i) the coldest weather?
   ii) the warmest weather?

4 a) Explain why there are large currents flowing in the oceans, such as those shown in Figure 3.

  b) Which major current affects the climate in Britain?

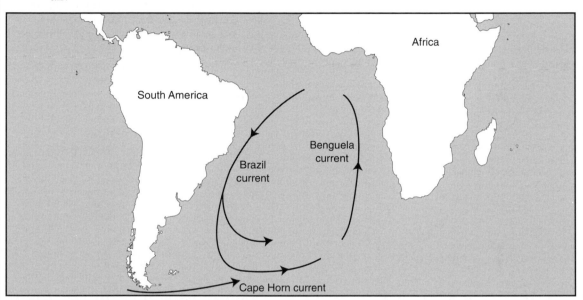

Figure 3

5 You arrive on the beach and place your deckchair looking out to sea. A sea breeze blows into your face; as the Sun sets you feel a gentle breeze blowing on your back. Explain these observations.

6 India experiences two monsoons each year; one is wet and one is dry (see Figure 4).

  a) The south-west monsoon is wet. Explain why.

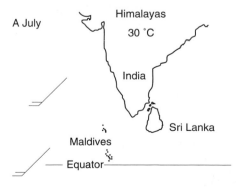
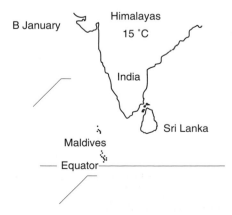

Figure 4

b) What causes the wind to blow from the south-west in July?

c) Why is the January monsoon dry?

d) James wants to visit the Maldives. The average temperature there is 30 °C all year. Does it matter when he goes?

7 Figure 5A shows sunlight falling on the Earth.

A

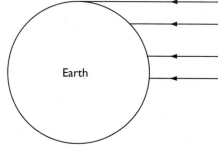

Earth

B

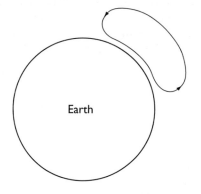

Earth

Figure 5

a) Explain why it is much hotter at the Equator than at the poles.

Figure 5B shows how convection currents might occur on an Earth which did not rotate.

b) i) Explain the direction of the currents.
   ii) Make a copy of the diagram and add three more possible currents.

c) In fact convection currents on the Earth are more complicated. Draw a diagram to show polar, mid-latitude and tropical convection cells. What causes these three cells to exist rather than just one?

8 In the Martian summer, temperatures on the surface vary from -120 °C at the poles to $+20$ °C near the Equator. Explain how these temperature extremes might contribute to the violent dust storms observed on the planet's surface.

9 Figure 6 shows how hot air rises near the Equator and flows either towards the north or south.

a) Explain why the air is deflected east.

b) When the air cools it falls back to the surface of the Earth and flows back towards the Equator. This gives rise to the prevailing winds. Make a diagram to show the direction of the prevailing winds near to the Equator.

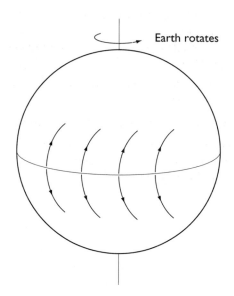

Earth rotates

Figure 6 Hot air rising near the Equator is deflected towards the east.

10 After a sunny day in winter, the temperature drops very rapidly in the evening.

a) Why does the temperature drop rapidly?

b) Explain why dew and fog are likely to form on such a day, especially if the ground has been moist.

11 a) What is an isobar?

b) What do the numbers mean in Figures 7 A and B?

A

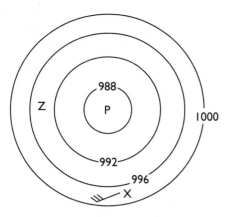

B

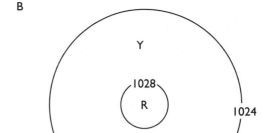

Figure 7

Both weather systems P and R are in the northern hemisphere.

c) i) What types of weather systems are P and R?
   ii) Explain what type of weather each brings.

d) What direction does the wind blow at (i) Y (ii) Z?

e) Estimate the wind speeds at Y and Z.

a) Explain where you can see (i) a warm front (ii) a cold front (iii) an occluded front.

b) Draw a vertical section to show how the frontal system looks along the line XY.

c) Make a weather forecast for (i) Edinburgh and (ii) Birmingham for the next 24 hours. In your answer you should mention: clouds, temperature, rainfall, wind speed and direction.

12 Figure 8 shows a frontal system approaching Britain, travelling eastwards from the Atlantic.

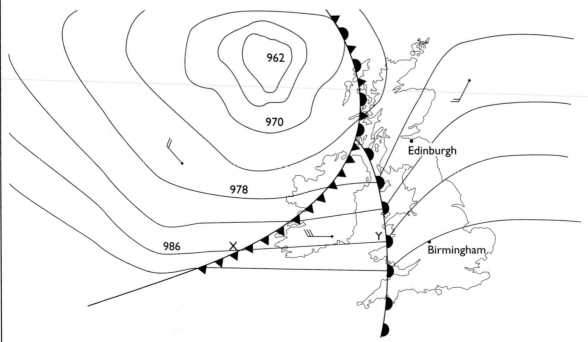

Figure 8

125